LEADING PEOPLE:

LEARNING FROM PEOPLE

Lessons from education

professionals

**Judith Bell and
Bernard T. Harrison**

OPEN UNIVERSITY PRESS
Buckingham · Philadelphia

Open University Press
Celtic Court
22 Ballmoor
Buckingham
MK18 1XW

email: enquiries@openup.co.uk
world wide web: http://www.openup.co.uk

and
325 Chestnut Street
Philadelphia, PA 19106, USA

First Published 1998

A catalogue record of this book is available from the British Library

ISBN   0 335 20074 5 (pb)   0 335 20075 3 (hb)

Library of Congress Cataloging-in-Publication Data
Bell, Judith, 1930–
    Leading people, learning from people : lessons from education professionals / Judith Bell, Bernard T. Harrison.
        p.   cm.
    Includes bibliographical references and index.
    ISBN 0–335–20075–3 (hardcover). – ISBN 0–335–20074–5 (pbk.)
    1. School improvement programs – Great Britain.   2. School improvement programs – Australia.   3. School supervision – Great Britain.   4. School supervision – Australia.   5. Educational leadership – Great Britain.   6. Educational leadership – Australia. I. Harrison, Bernard T.   II. Title.
    LB2822.84.G7B45   1998
        371.2'00941–dc21   98–13869
                                                                                          CIP

Typeset by Graphicraft Limited, Hong Kong
Printed in Great Britain by Biddles Ltd, Guildford and King's Lynn

CONTENTS

LIST OF FIGURES

ACKNOWLEDGEMENTS

We have received a great deal of assistance in the production of this book from friends and experienced practitioners, many of whom have read our scripts, corrected our misunderstandings and offered helpful suggestions as to how our drafts might be improved. We should like to thank Colin Jones, Stockport and High Peak Training and Enterprise Council; Sarah Pearce, of Investors in People UK; and Peter Skinner, of Understanding British Industry, for providing us with publications and names of key practitioners relating to the Investors in People programme. Also Ian McNay, Professor of Education at the University of Greenwich, who, as always, responded to a request for help in locating materials which had eluded detection from our unfruitful searches.

Very particular thanks to Glad Capewell, Director of Curriculum Planning at the Ridge College in Stockport; Judy Hope, Personnel Manager at Barnsley College in Yorkshire; Chris Parkin, Senior Adviser, Education Services, South and East Cheshire Training and Enterprise Council; Jan Dominey, Education and Management Consultant; and Colin Williams-Powell, Director of Human Resources at the Boys' and Girls' Welfare Society in Cheadle, Stockport – all of whom gave a great deal of time to talk about their experiences of the Investors in People Initiative and/or to read and comment on drafts of Chapter 4.

Similar thanks to Maurice Mealing, education consultant and former member of Her Majesty's Inspectorate; Dr Elaine Millard, who lectures in Education at the University of Sheffield; and Dr Esmeralda Brodeth, librarian at the University of Bethlehem, who also agreed to read drafts and, again, provided guidance about ways in which certain chapters might be improved.

Important support and advice has been provided by many Australian colleagues. These include, especially, Robin Clarke, President of the Western Australian Secondary Principals' Association (WASPA), who gave invaluable advice on access to Western Australian schools and staff; Dr Moreton Harslett, formerly District Superintendent of Schools in Western Australia and now Senior Research Fellow at Edith Cowan University; Ken Wyatt, Dr Gary Partington, Kaye Richer and Dr John Godfrey, members of the Edith Cowan University (ECU) Research Project on Aboriginal Student Retention and Motivation; Dr Susan Hill and Dr Michael Harvey, members of the ECU Research Project on Professional Development for School Leaders; Lena Donskyj, who provided a co-ordinating role between the UK-based and Australian-based authors; and Alison Cheetham who solved seemingly unsolvable problems – and actually made the complexities of wordprocessing seem easy.

Finally, a word about those who allowed us to write about their experiences, but who, for reasons which will become apparent, wish to remain anonymous. They have provided insights into some key difficulties facing teachers and managers in all sectors of education today. In some chapters, in an effort to ensure anonymity, we have changed titles, names of posts held, types of institution, department or subject area – at the request of the people involved. We cannot thank them enough for their openness, honesty and generosity. We can only hope we have done justice to their experiences.

To all of you, our most grateful thanks.

Judith Bell
Bernard T. Harrison

PREFACE

Since the mid-1980s, we have been involved in research and consultancy visits to schools, colleges and universities and have taught on advanced studies programmes for experienced educators in the UK, Australia, South-east Asia, Trinidad and elsewhere. Our work has included visits to other organizations, public and private, which have provided opportunities for useful comparisons of practice in different contexts. We have been struck by the fact that in some institutions, staff morale is at a low ebb, and there is little sense of direction, academic or otherwise, whereas in others, located in similar cultural and social settings, staff appear to enjoy their work and to have retained their commitment to providing the best possible learning experience for students. We began to ask why this was. Why, in institutions and departments which face similar problems, are some considered to be 'failing' whereas others are 'succeeding'?

We accept that there will never be one single solution to major problems, but we are convinced that some useful answers may emerge from the analysis of and commentary on our direct observation of the experiences of teachers and leaders in educational settings. We have tried, above all, to focus on what *is*, rather than what *ought to be*. What actually happens when people are managed well, and when they are managed badly? What happens to people when things go wrong, as they inevitably do from time to time, even in the best schools, colleges and universities? What kinds of actions by teachers and their leaders actually work?

We decided to ask a range of people in different educational settings and at different stages in their careers to talk to us about such questions as these, and to allow us to observe them in action during their working day.

The studies in this book reflect their experience. Predictably, perhaps, their major concerns centred on the quality of leadership, and the ways in which people were enabled (or were frustrated in their attempts) to achieve their best work. Their accounts include frank examples of sometimes heroic feats of ingenuity, fortitude or forbearance on the part of managers and also of those who were managed. They include reflections on times when things failed to go to plan. Those reflections dwell, for example, on what precisely is involved in dealing with the imperfections, as well as potential for good, of the people involved.

The following chapters record their successes, and in a few cases, their failures in confronting difficult situations, in coping with change, and in achieving (or failing to achieve) a collaborative working environment. Several of the chapters show how difficulties can arise if individuals, within or outside the school, college or university, put their own goals and value priorities before what is perceived by colleagues as being the common good. If that happens, then educational leaders need to draw on all their reserves to maintain morale, to find ways of sustaining team and individual effort, to maintain their own enthusiasm and direction, and no matter how turbulent the times, to ensure continuing quality of provision for students. That is quite a task and it is hardly surprising that not all managers succeed, all of the time, in avoiding conflict.

Our cases are based in schools, colleges and in university departments in England and in Australia, all of which are now facing remarkably similar challenges. The context, size and geographical location might be different, but the issues have proved to be much the same.

1

INDIVIDUALS AND INSTITUTIONS: THE SOLOISTS IN THE ORCHESTRA

In this chapter, we consider some of the challenges facing individuals and institutions, as they cope with fundamental change. To meet those challenges, we propose collaboration as an essential guiding principle for continuous school and college improvement. Collaboration to achieve successful outcomes for education involves the whole profession, and includes all its community and government stakeholders. Throughout the complex network of education, collaboration extends from small teams in schools and colleges, to government level efforts to get education provision right. At its best, collaboration integrates, rather than excludes, individual talents; it ensures that the orchestra has the full benefit of all its individual players, who are committed to working in harmony.

Developing teams that make it happen

Our approach to people management will come as no surprise to those who believe that people are an organization's most precious resource. Morgan (1988) quoted this advice by an experienced senior executive in *Riding the Waves of Change*, who had no doubt about the value of people:

> It all boils down to one thing, people, people, people, people, people. I don't care what country, or what organization, or what team you are in – it is the people and whether you can organize those people to achieve an end that counts. If you have the right people in all your key sectors, and all of your people are keen then you will make it happen.
>
> (Morgan 1988: 55–6)

However, this executive recognized that it is not just a matter of choosing the right individuals; the collective group needs also to be 'right'. He continued:

> Two organizations can agree to go through the same process and get the same consultants to help them, but the difference in effectiveness rests in the ability of those present to get into the issues that need to be discussed.
>
> (ibid.)

In his view, high quality individuals and high quality teams are interdependent. The hard currency, he believed, is excellence:

> I want all my people to be excellent. In today's competitive environment that's exactly what has to happen. Everyone has to be damn good, and we have to make it pull together.
>
> (ibid.)

All our experience in education has led us to support the view that the integrated components in a synergized team are inevitably of greater value than the separate parts. Excellence does not happen by chance. Individuals need support, encouragement and opportunities to develop; this means that the task of leaders and managers is to strive continuously for excellence in their dealings with people, even if they never quite achieve it. Where people are successfully engaged in making change happen – which involves much more than conforming to management edicts – then organizations will really move. Agreeing in principle to a reform is an important first stage; but it is in trying to achieve the stage where all 'those present' are ready to 'get into the issues that need to be discussed', that managers are really put to the test. Where teams are engaged in genuine dialogue there is, as Senge (1994) showed, a free flow of communication that involves continuous development through learning.

Coleman, writing in *The Australian* (23 April 1997), suggested that poorly performing organizations often share two intriguing characteristics, both of which act as blocks against 'getting into the issues'. The first of these is a 'denial mode', where it is argued, erroneously, that what is done is best practice and cannot possibly be done differently. Inevitably, denial mode resists any frank evaluation of problems, and any moves towards strategic change.

The second characteristic is a 'tendency to react to events', which can paralyse organizations by 'throwing them into near permanent crisis with never-ending reviews'. Reaction mode, Coleman argued, 'comes from an inability to look ahead, . . . to identify threats that could be faced, or to invent a competitor or situation that is their worst nightmare and ensure it could be faced successfully'. Reactive organizations may seem to be exciting places, compared to the 'boring' predictability of a well-run organization. Yet reactive behaviour leads, typically, to waste, not to improvement.

Sometimes it has been government itself which has led to a reactive rush of lemmings, as was exemplified in the overhasty and overbearing handling of UK curriculum reform in the late 1980s and early 1990s, which led to the inevitable review and partial dismantling of the curriculum over a number of years. As with other organizations, government too can abuse its powers, when 'people lack accountability for results and have a near psychopathic ability to ignore the ethical consequences of their actions' (Coleman 1997).

The lives of people, individually and in organizations, are governed by assumptions and principles. These are likely to change from time to time, but cannot be subject to the sudden whims of individuals, even when the individual happens to be a chief executive. When there is a risk of collision with these principles, it may be people who need to change course, rather than principles. This is memorably illustrated through a perception shifting experience, related by Frank Koch, which happened during his service in the US Navy, and which appeared in an in-house Navy journal:

Two battleships assigned to the training squadron had been at sea on maneuvers in heavy weather for several days. I was serving on the lead battleship and was on watch on the bridge as night fell. The visibility was poor with patchy fog, so the captain remained on the bridge keeping an eye on all activities.

Shortly after dark, the lookout on the wing of the bridge reported, 'Light bearing on the starboard bow'.

'Is it steady or moving astern?' the captain called out.

Lookout replied, 'Steady, captain,' which meant we were on a dangerous collision course with that ship.

The captain then called to the signalman, 'Signal that ship. We are on a collision course, advise you change course 20 degrees.'

Back came a signal, 'Advisable for you to change course 20 degrees'.

The captain said, 'Send, I'm a captain, change course 20 degrees.'

'I'm a seaman second class,' came the reply. 'You had better change course 20 degrees.'

By that time, the captain was furious. He spat out, 'Send, I'm a battleship. Change course 20 degrees.'

Back came the flashing light, 'I'm a lighthouse.'

We changed course.

(quoted in Covey 1990: 33)

One–nil to the seaman second class in his lighthouse, who saved the ship by daring to challenge an unacceptable command.

Vicious circles? Or virtuous circles?

Without knowing the source of the following quotation, how should a reader respond to it?

I do not know what is happening in Australia now, but in Britain teaching has become an under-regarded profession. There is a vicious circle at work. The worse schools become the more reluctant good people are to become teachers; the fewer good people who become teachers, the worse schools become. The well-publicized problems of inner-city schools, the indiscipline and the disinclination to take learning seriously, deter people from teaching as a career.

This view of today's schools is, in one sense, only too familiar. It reflects decades-long criticism of public education – informed, partly informed or ill informed – that has been voiced, by media, political and community groups. In another sense, however, the view is remarkable, since it was written by an educationist, who represents a distinctive, though influential minority within education. It is taken from a keynote address by Eric Anderson (1995: 12–13) to a restricted international colloquium on education. Before becoming rector at Lincoln College, Oxford, Anderson served as headmaster at Abingdon, Shrewsbury and Eton public schools. In his address he advocated that education should 'start with great men, great events and great writers' (p. 9) – which echoes, curiously, Kenneth Baker's view of history as expounded when he was secretary of state for education during the implementation period of the Education Reform Act 1988. Anderson declared, too, that schools should once more become 'what Dr Johnson defined in his Dictionary as – "houses of discipline and instruction" ' (p. 13).

Anderson's assertion that schools are getting worse represents, to say the least, a disputable view of British schools in the 1990s (or, for that matter, of Australian schools). Yet it serves to illustrate how members of an influential intelligentsia can, themselves, be tempted to commit simple errors of logical inference, when slipping from discussing teaching as 'an under-regarded profession' to making quaint and tendentious claims about the 'vicious circle' of worsening schools and teachers. There may seem to be little point in trying to engage in reasonable argument with a view that seems so empty of evidence – and which also lacks acknowledgement that, as an educator, the author might have been directly implicated in what has gone wrong. Whatever music the rest of the educational orchestra may have begun to practise, this particular player seems reluctant to change the old tune.

Eric Anderson's view may be unjust or, at least, out of date. Yet it has to be admitted that such views have been persistent and widely voiced. While these continue, schools face, at the very least, an urgent task of communication with their communities. If they are better than Anderson alleged, then they need to show that they are doing good work, that they are making a real difference for their students, and that they are on a course for continuous improvement. Throughout the world, parents have shown that they want the schools to which they send their children to be, if not 'houses of discipline and instruction', then certainly to be safe, orderly places, where children gain evident benefit from teaching and learning.

As with all of today's organizations, the pressure is on schools and colleges to reform. Krell and Spich (1996: 59) have suggested that 'environmental pressures are diverse, multiple and changing. Increased complexity, uncertainty, risk and interdependence seem to be the reigning conditions'. Yet the views expressed by Anderson are shared by parents and politicians who, sensing that something is wrong with education, are tempted sometimes to put the clock back, not forward. It is, for them, an understandable reaction (though unlikely to help, in terms of finding solutions), to recall an allegedly ideal past, which might match their own favourite school memories. Meanwhile, let it be admitted that some schools have, themselves, clung uncritically to existing frameworks, refusing to accommodate changes in the world around them.

Seeking to explain this, Hough and Paine (1997: 102) take a lesson from evolutionary biology, in comparing the relative survival chances of the wildebeest with the impala. The wildebeest has adapted to specific conditions within tightly defined boundaries, and is adversely affected by environmental change, whereas the impala thrives on a variety of food sources. In contrast to the 'flexible and adaptive' impala,

> Many schools are like the wildebeest. They are the creations of the industrial era, adapted in many ways to the needs of such a society. But that society is rapidly disappearing into the past. Schools now need to be more like the impala, adaptive rather than adapted. As the environments of schools change as we move into the information era . . . schools as Learning Communities need to become adaptive systems that continually renew themselves and create their own futures. Schools can become dynamic, creative and adaptive by unleashing creative individuals and teams within a . . . shared sense of purpose and a shared sense of what we stand for.
>
> (Hough and Paine 1997: 102)

A brief historical note on the UK scene since the late 1980s may help to explain how new insights such as these have emerged at considerable cost, sometimes, to reform minded educationists who have actually tried to put wrong things right in education. This has been a difficult task, during times when hostile government and community attitudes have joined, not in collaboration, but in complicated battle with the teaching profession's own resistance to embrace change.

The 1988 Act: a device for collaboration or for division?

The Education Reform Act 1988 resulted in the greatest amount of education legislation ever known, but for two or more years before then, it had become apparent that government was concerned at what it saw as a lowering of standards in schools and colleges.

Evidence was in short supply, but secretaries of state for education 'knew' that teachers were not doing a sufficiently good job and must be made to do better. They were supported in that view when a series of damaging reports appeared during the 1970s and 1980s, which related to a number of obviously failing schools; several of these reports resulted in judicial enquiries and court cases (Auld 1976). In the opinion of ministers, it was clear that teachers, principals, teacher educators and local education authorities could no longer be trusted to provide students with a sound education.

Let it be conceded that this heavy-hammer government approach was, in part, the profession's own fault. Many educators knew that there were indifferent to poor teachers in our schools, colleges and universities, but they held on to the fact that most teachers worked hard and did their utmost for their students. Over the years, teachers' unions had consistently refused to cooperate with government over any external interference in the curriculum. The 'secret garden of the curriculum' had reigned supreme. The tone was, 'Keep out of our patch. Teachers know what education is all about, and you don't. Teacher autonomy is paramount'.

Members of Her Majesty's Inspectorate (HMI) knew that all was not well, but had no powers to close a school, nor to take action about poor teaching. That was the role of the school headteacher and the local education authority (LEA), yet they rarely took action. Finally, ministers lost patience and said 'If you cannot sort out your own problems, we shall do it for you'. Thereafter, teachers experienced some of their most turbulent and exhausting years in living memory. Conditions of service were changed. A national curriculum (which proved impossible to deliver) was announced and, with it, tests for children aged 7, 11 and 14. It was promised at first that the results of these tests would not be published, but then it was promised that they would. League tables of GCSE and A level results were to be published in order to 'prove' which schools were good schools and which were not. The publication of these raw results was, arguably, more unjust than any other government action at the time. HM Inspectorate was disbanded and a new Inspectorate established, the new version to have teeth. Inspection reports were to be published, so that all might see which schools were 'bad'.

Schools and colleges had been accustomed to being inspected by HMI, but in universities HMI had ventured only into specialized areas. Now, universities were also assessed or audited; university staff found it hard to accept that outsiders were actually going to sit in their classes, and give them a grade to indicate the quality of their teaching. Whatever next? However, the rules were clear. There was no choice, since the grading given influenced the budget and the permitted student numbers. Similar legislation continued into the 1990s. The bruises were still evident late into the 1990s. It would be easy to take the view that all the legislation introduced over that turbulent period was bad or unnecessary, but gradually evidence began to emerge that the new procedures were in some cases showing signs of improving the quality of teaching and learning, though at a price for those involved.

There was a new awareness of variation in standards, and increasing numbers of teachers themselves began to ask, for example, why some schools consistently performed badly (on reasonable criteria) whereas others in the same socio-economic area performed consistently well. What is wrong in parents having information about the values, curriculum, teaching methods and even test results of schools in their area so that they can make an informed choice about the best school for their children? Why should one maverick school have the power to deprive students of access to mathematics, science or even English? (HMI had in fact found a few such cases in the UK).

Since parts of the 1988 Act made reasonable sense, what went wrong with it? One of the main problems was the speed with which it was introduced and the timescale for implementation. There was no time to evaluate one new initiative before managers and teachers were confronted by others. Teachers were buried in paper to such an extent that much of it was never read. The forests of the world were decimated because of the 1988 Act and by ongoing legislation.

There was insufficient funding for the purchase of new materials. Consultation time was limited, and little note taken of some very genuine concerns. But perhaps the most debilitating effect of the Education Reform Act 1988 and all the publicity and reports which followed was the frequently repeated message that teachers were doing a bad job and must be made to do better. Education managers must be more efficient and be more willing to adopt the techniques common in industry. And the message was reinforced over and over again. The outcome was that collaboration, along with goodwill, flew out the window.

Gradually, however, the voice of reason came to be heard. Ron Dearing (not a politician and now Lord Dearing,) was appointed to establish committees which had good teacher representation and which tried, during the early 1990s, to simplify and make workable the National Curriculum and other provisions of the Act. At last, the orchestra was invited to engage in teamwork, instead of being misled by individualists from the right or the left of the political spectrum.

In May 1997 a new government was elected in the UK, with a declared mission to work with common purpose to improve the quality of its schools. The policies of government are, of necessity, a key component in any new mission but the new government showed no signs of a lessening of control, nor of understanding that the external imposition of bureaucratic top-down plans and systems will rarely be received with enthusiasm by those who are required to implement them. Governments of many countries, alarmed at the escalating costs of education and the lack of control over the nature of provision, have imposed planning systems linked to funding, in the belief that

> performance in the public sector can only be improved . . . by making public organizations and their management look as much like the private sector as possible. Good managers have the same tasks and duties whatever sector they are in. Indeed, the accelerating introduction of market-led competition to organize the provision of public services is intended to dissolve the boundary between public and private provision.
>
> (Ranson and Stewart 1994: 26)

The education sector was not, perhaps, always as efficient as it might have been. Its management skills may have been sometimes rudimentary. Perhaps some educators deplored the notion of marketing their institutions, or adopting the principles and instruments of performance management. They were busy getting on with the demanding job of teaching and researching and, to be fair, in the past, they were never asked to perform as if they were running a factory. A typical stance among educationists has been: 'we are dealing with human beings, not cans of peas or cars, and that makes our institutions totally different from industry where profit is paramount'.

For the future, though, schools, colleges and universities have no choice but to conform to government and community requirements for more precise planning, goal setting and financial control. Staff have to be accountable not only to themselves and to their students, but also to governors, parents and government auditors.

Education managers have had to learn new skills, many of which are common practice in industry and commerce. Why should it not be so? No one would question the need to be efficient and effective, would they? Yet it would seem to be folly to attempt to operate an educational institution successfully, if goals were to be set only by senior managers who took little account of the skills and value priorities of people in the organization.

Interestingly, government demands in the late 1980s and early 1990s, for a more rationalist approach to planning in education, took place at a time when some private sector organizations began to challenge their own hierarchical structures, and to question the effectiveness of systems which take no account of the varied values and personal goals of the people who work there. They experimented with learning teams, and with flatter structures, in order to encourage initiative throughout the organization. There were some notable successes in establishing problem-solving teams which included not only high level professionals, but also relatively junior members of organizations who, in some cases, had never been consulted before and whose input proved to be invaluable (see, for example, Arcaro 1995; Harrison *et al.* 1995).

Even so, many management theorists still continued to play down the importance of individual differences and the contribution that people can make to the organization. In Herriot's (1992: 58) view, 'perhaps they did so because their underlying purpose was to help organizations devise systems which treated employees alike. You can design work or reward systems which apply across the board only if you assume that people want the same things out of work'. Yet, he continues, that is clearly not the case:

> They bring all their individual differences with them, especially their differences in values. Organizations will utterly fail to understand employees' expectations unless they realize that:
>
> - employees have *different value priorities* from each other, though there will be groups whose values are similar
> - they often have different value priorities *at different stages of their careers and their lives*
> - those with the power in organizations are likely to *misperceive the value priorities of others*
> - value priorities have *changed* in general over the past few years and are likely to continue to do so.
>
> (Herriot 1992: 58–9)

These differences in priorities are likely to be particularly evident in education. The title of this chapter recalls a television interview with the conductor of a famous English chamber orchestra. The interviewer suggested that conducting such an orchestra where all members were soloists in their own right must be very pleasurable. The conductor agreed; but, he said, there could also be problems, because each one of them thought they knew better than he did how the music should be interpreted. They also made quite sure he knew why their approach was infinitely better than his. It was, he said, a matter of negotiation.

Educational institutions are much the same. All members of staff are likely to be well qualified, as 'soloists' in their own particular specialist area. They inevitably have views about how the institution should be run, and strong opinions about their position in it. Their beliefs and performance may be in direct conflict with those of management, so how is agreement (or, at least, consensus) to be reached? If all soloists hold firm, the concert will never take place.

Murgatroyd and Morgan (1992), writing about schools, had little doubt that it is the responsibility of management to educate the institution's stakeholders in strategic planning:

> Many attempts at a specific strategy fail because of the inability of senior management to secure prior consent for the strategy from the rank and file of teachers, and to talk through and agree the sort of additional commitments the strategy would impose. In short, ownership of the strategy by all key stakeholders has not been secured.
>
> ... all aspects of the school must be designed in such a way as to fit this strategy or reflect it. This includes recruitment and training of teachers, purchase decisions for learning and service resources, equipment purchases, marketing of the school, the design of communication systems within the school and between the school and its stakeholders, the development of pedagogy, the work of management, links with industry and government and so on. It is important that the school regards itself as active in its pursuit of strategy, so that everyone concerned with the school will sense the commitment of people to the strategy. This takes vision, communication, culture building and teamwork.
>
> (Murgatroyd and Morgan 1992: 39)

All this is easier said than done. Bemused managers might well ask how, constructively, to take account of different values in strategic planning and in goal setting, and still to obtain 'prior consent to the strategy'? How can they ensure that the individuals who make up the whole have the opportunity to achieve their full potential, to make a full contribution to the success of the institution, but at the same time not lose sight of their own values? And, as will be illustrated in Chapter 2, what if the values of individuals conflict so strongly with the desired culture of the institution as to cause total breakdown in the planning and delivery process? After all, planning cannot be a chaotic free-for-all, with determined individuals and groups standing in the way of necessary change. Not every view expressed and every objection raised can be adopted.

We have known a few individuals who, on principle, never agree with anything proposed by 'management'. So, in the end, are senior managers likely to say, 'A plague on all your houses. What I say goes'? Do they revert to a rationalist rather than consultative approach? Being a people-aware manager is not the same as being weak and agreeing with everyone. At some stage, decisions have to be made, some of which may be unpopular, as is graphically illustrated in some of the following chapters. Then, the reality, the strain and even the feasibility of consultative people management and team building is really put to the test.

Some leaders may find themselves on a collision course with their colleagues, as happened in the case of the ship's captain and the seaman second class and his lighthouse; and sometimes – as in the case of the captain – they will be wrong. Fortunately, most of us are not usually in the critical position of a sea captain in patchy fog. We may be allowed some failures, as long as we do not sink the ship, and as long as we are willing to learn from our mistakes and the mistakes and successes of others.

How collaborative teams can work

In applying good practice from quality teamwork in the private sector, Hough and Paine (1997: 179–80) identified three kinds of key teams in schools and colleges: the *leading learning team* (responsible for strategic management planning and evaluation); the *task learning team* (where staff are empowered to design new processes and systems to enhance continuous improvement); and *teaching-learning* teams (which include teachers teaching and designing learning programmes, as well as students involved in co-operative learning). As process/quality circles, each of which represents an essential function of the school/college, these teams are interconnected; good communication among them is essential for their success. Hough and Paine (1997: 181) invoke the notion of 'procedural justice', in arguing that 'leaders must do everything in their power to make sure that their decisions are fair and seen to be fair'. In the daily operations of managing people in a school, college or department, it is difficult to imagine a more important principle than this.

Hough and Paine (1997: 181) cite research that led to the Duran rule: 'Whenever there is a problem 85 per cent of the time it will be the system, and 15 percent of the time it will be the worker'. This rule requires that managers should always scrutinize the problem first, not the person. Only when the 85 per cent possibility has been exhausted, should the manager turn to the worker, in order to ask (a) whether they actually want to perform better, and (b) whether they are competent to improve their performance. Yet, even though the great majority of a staff may understand the need for change, managers must still handle the phenomenon of staff resistance to change. Hough and Paine (1997: 185) refer to a US survey in 1992 of Fortune 500 executives, who reported that 'only about half of their change efforts had been successful. They cited employer resistance as the major obstacle in 76 per cent of cases'. An implication for the conductor/educational manager who wishes to introduce new ways of playing, is that not only individual soloists, but also whole sections of the orchestra/school may be reluctant to play.

Clearly, it is not enough for managers just to have good sense on their side. One of our headteacher interviewees, speaking in a remote rural Australian context, summed up the essential requirements for her job: 'You do need a good head for this job – but you also need a good supply of heart; and, believe me, you need balls. You need all of these on your teacher teams, too'. We have found no successful managers in any organizations who would disagree with that. Individual leaders and collaborative teams alike need to be strong in cool reflection, analysis and critical judgement. They also need an emotional willingness to accommodate the otherness of other people, with all the resources of patience, support, encouragement, willingness to listen and negotiate and so on, that this involves. As Martin Buber declared, 'The opposite of compulsion is not freedom but bonding' (in Yoshida 1994: 89).

As for the third quality, which might be defined politely as 'courage under fire', all leaders and teams will, when the going gets rough, face unpopularity and loss of support. While such times always require some self-inspection ('Are we really doing this the right way?') there is clearly no point in calling oneself a leader if resolve collapses under pressures that do not, of themselves, offer better arguments or better justice.

On the need for heart, in a practical investigation of collaborative leadership in schools, Telford (1995: 124) offered a distillation of causal links in the collaboration of teacher-leaders, teachers and students, which constitutes 'the *heart* of the collaborative milieu, and what it is, in *essence*, that brings about school success'. Building on earlier typologies, she identified four dominant factors that contribute to success through collaboration, two of which concern people, and two of which reflect the whole school/college:

1 development of the educational potential of students
2 professional development of teachers
3 good organizational health
4 institutionalization of vision.

Telford's comments on the first two of these factors dwell on the 'head' aspect of good teamwork – the need for planning, for good systems, for an innovative curriculum. The third factor depends on the 'heart' – 'harmonious relationships . . . a cordial, congenial and supportive working environment' (Telford 1995: 125). And the fourth factor requires the courage and will of leaders and teams to enable a 'collective reinforcing of the guiding values and attitudes of the school' (ibid.). As we have argued elsewhere (Bell and Harrison 1995), having a vision is crucial; but it will have little impact unless it is brought down to earth, and grounded in daily school/college practice.

Although new kinds of collaborative teams were emerging in the late 1980s and were operating in many schools and colleges by the mid-1990s, research into their processes and achievements remains patchy. Wallace and Hall (1994) provided a notable study of senior management teams (SMTs) in operation in secondary schools, which highlighted 'strains' as well as 'gains' that need to be understood by school/college managers. Most prominent among those 'strains' was the destructive impact that a dysfunctional member of a team can make, unless checked or, if necessary, unless excluded altogether.

The scope of these new teams has been ambitious, in that team members deal 'not only with specific educational problems but also with the dynamics of change itself' (Maeroff 1993: 19). A contribution to research into teacher teams, which highlighted the delicate interstices of genuinely functional team networking, was recorded by Engeström (1994: 59). His findings, about the ways in which functional teacher teams succeed in helping all members to advance their thinking through exploratory discussion, have interesting echoes of earlier work by Barnes and others on exploratory talking and writing (see, for example, Harrison 1996: 11–14). Engeström (1994: 59) summed up the recurring pattern of the teacher team discourse that he observed as 'a spiral or a "potter's wheel" with constant circling back and repetition of issues. This pattern was not consciously problematized or developed – it functioned as if "behind the backs" of the participants'. Engeström moves from the potter's wheel analogy, to compare team discourse with the music of an orchestra: 'The mediating instruments used by the participants were primarily linguistic, conditional strings being the most prominent among them'. The constant reflective discourse, 'before, during and after action' is the same process as the 'mediating strings' of players who are attuned to the main orchestral music (Engeström 1994: 59).

Collaborating with learners

To care for learners is to put care for their academic and whole progress as the top priority for a school or college. Inevitably, any reform agenda for education will raise concerns among committed educationists, about the impact of reforms on learners, as one headteacher discloses:

> When I began my teaching career, we would gently mock our head (but not to her face), when she made solemn remarks about the pupils being a 'precious cargo'. But we also believed her. I am afraid, though, that we've been tempted, in recent years, to see pupils increasingly as resource units, whose success or failure in examinations reflects well or badly on the school and the staff. Without losing the gains that we have made, we must start again to think first about people, both pupils and staff. Then schools might become the worthwhile and civilized places that I think they should always aim to be.
>
> (headteacher, quoted in Harrison 1998)

This headteacher admits her concerns that, during the education reforms of the late 1980s and early 1990s, an overpreoccupation with systems grew in the management of education. This might, if left unchecked, have endangered the quality of teacher–learner relations and, it would follow, the quality of learning itself. Whatever the justification for the new climate that emerged, and for its accompanying new systems, it remains of first concern that learners at all stages – children, adolescents, young and mature adults – need to be understood for *who* they are.

Teachers, at all levels, know that they must get this right, not least, for their own professional sakes. Nixon (1997: 92), for example, discussing the encroachments of managerialism in the academic workplace, acknowledged Halsey's (1992) argument that new 'material and ideological conditions . . . are transforming university teachers into a new proletariat'. If this was occurring in what were still comparatively privileged conditions of higher education, what must have happened in the schools? Nixon envisages, however, the regeneration of a 'new professionalism constructed around the notion of the university teacher as educator' (1997: 100). This important notion of a 'new professionalism' will be considered in Chapter 7. For the present, we note Nixon's emphasis on the quality of teaching and learning, as a crucial factor in the new professionalism. To enter into a full client relationship with learners is to collaborate with them, and also to promote conditions for collaboration among learners themselves. Paradoxically, this emphasis on team or community patterns in learning must involve, in the words of a practising teacher, 'Honouring diversity. Every child, every teacher is different. So we try to create a family setting in the classroom where we are all accepted for our uniqueness' (quoted in Wood 1993: 28). As was shown in a range of accounts from diverse professional areas, including medicine, law, accountancy and politics (Broadbent *et al.* 1997), this sensitivity to individual client needs has become an important issue for all areas of work that involve people. Moreover, expertise gained in any of these areas can be applied elsewhere. For example, Charlton and Dewdney's *The Mediator's Handbook* (1995) was written for legal practitioners; yet the accounts of effective mediation that this book provides, all of which are described as 'unique', demonstrate patterns that are common in all professional interactions with people. They are readily applicable to education, where teachers require good mediation skills in their work with learners, parents and all others involved in the life of the school or college. One of the most difficult things in the managing of people, after all, is to get each person not only to ventilate individual viewpoints, but also to acknowledge (though not necessarily agree) with 'the other viewpoint. Thus, the egocentric viewpoint is often filtered out as a normal result of the mediation process' (Charlton and Dewdney 1995: 145). However, no matter how skilful the mediation, firmly held values and principles can sometimes be impossible to change, as is illustrated in Chapter 2.

A collaborative culture will not be achieved overnight. As Evans and Panacek-Howell (1995: 39) concede, 'creating the optimum culture for change is an evolutionary process within the school environment where collaborative planning, and partnerships, collegial work, and reflective practice increasingly become the method by which all school business is done'. The actual processes of 'collaborative planning and partnerships . . . are more complex issues than they appear at first glance'. Advocating the need for inter-agency collaboration on behalf of whole families, Mellaville and Blank (1991: 18) argued that expertise and discipline in strategic planning depends crucially on high quality work among collaborative groups which can 'design and deliver services that are developmental rather than remedial . . . preventive rather than corrective in approach, and centred on the total needs of the child and family'.

Identifying essential competencies for collaboration

What, then, are the essential competencies that teachers and teacher-teams require for successful collaboration? Lists of competencies can, as Pollard and Tann warned (1993: 9) have their drawbacks, and may not be as long lasting as their inventors might hope. For example, regulations respecting the education of pupil teachers in 1846 included, among a number of now dated requirements, that pupils should know their catechism and that girl candidates should 'be able to sew neatly and to knit'. Even so, a well drawn up list of essential skills for a particular task can have its uses, so long as these are not then prescribed for eternity in tablets of stone. Wasley (1994: 205–6) drew on her observations of teachers to propose a list of twenty 'emerging characteristics of collaborating teachers'. She suggested that 'there is a growing need to redefine what it means to teach . . . I do not suggest a narrow, limiting definition but an expansive one, one that suggests growth and productivity'; she invited 'good debate and discussion' on her list, in the interests of clarification and agreement. Taking up that invitation, we offer this amended version of Wasley's list. Collaborative teachers and teacher teams

- share the *centre of the learning process with learners*
- attend to the *individual academic needs* of students, and use student performance as guides to their own effectiveness
- collaborate in *developing a diverse range of teaching/learning techniques* and are constantly improving their expertise here
- collaborate in promoting *connections* among students, parents, teachers and other community stakeholders
- collaborate in the *continuous improvement, through reshaping of the curriculum, and teaching and assessment of learning*
- are skilled in *exchanging (giving and receiving) constructive advice/ criticism* in all school/college contexts
- promote *the new professionalism through shared practice* with colleagues, learners, parents and others
- have clear *guiding principles* which are shared throughout the school/college: they know why they are doing what they are doing
- collaborate in *continuously examining school practices and structures* in the light of goals for students, and change these where appropriate
    (modified from Wasley 1994: 205–6, with acknowledgement)

In the same spirit as Wasley, we offer this list for further comment, amendment and improvement. The 'right' kinds of collaboration will, inevitably, lead to improvement through change, whereas the 'wrong' kinds (for example, staff 'sticking together' to resist change) can result only in a further victory for inertia. As Petterle (1993: 143) put it, 'the effective scuttling of change is actually the process of well-meaning individuals doing what they think is right for the profession, for the school, and for the children!' They are not, usually, villains, nor do they wish to be at all dysfunctional, yet their conspiracy can put the move towards improvement into full reverse – as is graphically illustrated in the following chapters.

2

THE CASE OF
A DEPARTMENT
UNDER THREAT:
THE CONVERGENCE
OF VALUES

There is no hiding the fact that educational provision is expensive and that costs are escalating; it was inevitable that governments in many countries and of different political persuasions would look for ways of halting the frightening spiralling of costs. 'Non-essential' education was an obvious target and adult education in the UK received particularly punitive cuts.

The case study in this chapter relates to one department of adult education in a large college of further education in the UK, which experienced great difficulties in conforming to new funding requirements. The identity of the college and the people involved have been disguised, and the accounts of certain confrontations have been modified at the request of those involved, but the nature of the problems facing the participants and the challenges they had to face have not.

The dilemma facing the department of adult education was that it offered very few accredited courses, and accreditation was required as a condition of funding at that time. The loss of funding meant that unless fundamental changes were implemented speedily, the department would be in serious difficulties.

The following account follows the progress of negotiation, the conflict of values and the challenges to deeply held beliefs which led to fundamental structural and curricular changes, though not without pain for the individuals concerned.

Background to adult education funding in the UK

For well over a hundred years, university departments of adult education/extramural studies in the UK were grant aided by central government for the provision of 'non-vocational liberal adult education', though the precise meaning of 'non-vocational' and 'liberal' was never spelt out. It was invariably taken to mean, among other things, that students would not be prepared for examinations. The departments were subject to inspection by HMI, albeit infrequently. The funding was ring-fenced and, therefore, safe from powerful predatory departments who generally felt their need was greater than that of a department which merely provided 'courses for old-age pensioners and bored housewives', to use their usual terminology. Staff in the departments were accustomed to such dismissive terminology and just carried on doing their job, which was to provide programmes of study for members of the public at a level deemed to be 'appropriate for a university', though, what was meant by this was never made clear. The fact that these departments were inspected by HMI was considered to be satisfactory evidence of the quality of provision – though that assumption was certainly questionable.

Funding for adult education in colleges of further education and adult centres was less secure and provision varied greatly in different parts of the UK, ranging from a great deal to none at all. In general, where there was provision, it followed the non-vocational liberal adult education paradigm, with strong resistance to the notion of accreditation and examination. When the financial cuts came in the early 1990s, they came with a vengeance in all sectors. The university providers, who had always felt confident that their funding would be safe, gradually woke up to the unpalatable fact that they had to conform to the requirements of central government or go out of business.

Adult centres and education departments in colleges were even more threatened by the new regulations. Ministers began to question the justification for providing public money to allow people to enjoy what they considered to be cheap courses for leisure time activities, in subjects which only occasionally resulted in some form of accreditation and which rarely provided actual evidence of quality. It was suggested that if people wanted to study 'for fun', they should pay.

Many adult educators took strong exception to the notion that they should be asked to provide such evidence. It was felt that some departments, such as engineering, might be able to provide suitable 'evidence' but non-vocational adult education was quite different. They stood their ground, found it difficult to believe their funding base could disappear almost overnight and assumed it would all be all right in the end. But the government meant business. New funding regulations virtually eliminated support for non-vocational liberal adult education which had been the *raison d'être* of their work for so many years.

Stage 1: Confronting the problem

One college principal, already burdened with cuts in the overall college budget, the looming prospect of staff redundancies and government demands for increased student numbers, regarded the threat to the adult education funding as just one more challenge to face in a life which appeared to consist of nothing but challenges. When the implications of the new regulations became clear, he met staff of the department to discuss what steps might be taken to salvage at least some of the existing work. As the programme stood at the time, it was his and the bursar's view that very little funding would be provided unless the department adopted an entirely new approach to adult education provision. This would involve a total review of the way the department was organized and the type of courses offered. The meeting lasted three hours. The adult educators had read the central government circulars, which in some cases were subject to various interpretations. They did not like what they read, but agreed to think about what might be done.

The meeting finished on a positive note, with everyone anxious to find some way out of the funding problem.

Stage 2: The inspection

The day after the meeting, as if the funding crises were not enough, the principal was notified that a full inspection of the college was planned by the Further Education Funding Council (FEFC). When HMI had full responsibility for inspecting schools, colleges and university departments of adult education, a report was produced, but was not made public. HMI could, and usually did advise, but though they might on some occasions make life difficult for the institutions if no action were taken on recommendations, they had little formal power. The new inspectors were very different. Their reports, which were published and available free of charge, pulled no punches. A bad report could have serious consequences and what was worse, the world would know if a college received low grades.

The principal was determined that the college would emerge well from the inspection. In order to ensure that any weaknesses were dealt with before the inspectors arrived, he invited a team of consultants to carry out a college review and to make any recommendations for improvement. The consultants spent two weeks talking to staff of all fifteen departments; they were not impressed by what they saw and heard in some cases. They were particularly critical of the department of adult education. They reported that outdated practices were impeding development and that though staff claimed they provided quality courses, they were unable to produce any actual evidence of quality. In their report, the consultants recommended that adult education and two other departments which were deemed to be ill prepared for the inspection should be asked to carry out a self-assessment exercise in order to

- consider the appropriateness of provision as it related to student need, inspection criteria, funding and curriculum regulations
- review the processes and procedures involved in the delivery of their programmes
- identify any gaps, anomalies or particular areas of weakness.

The principal decided there would be merit in asking *all* departments to carry out a review/self-assessment exercise rather than pointing the finger at departments identified as having major weaknesses, which would inevitably have caused resentment. No formal guidelines were provided, but it was stressed that judgements rather than descriptions would be required. It was made clear that all the returns would be confidential to the senior management team and that the exercise was simply a 'dry run' in preparation for the inspection.

Stage 3: The beginning of the arguments

Departments were not enthusiastic about having to delay what they saw as more urgent work in order to undertake the review, but after what had become the usual period of complaints about overwork, unnecessary bureaucracy and lack of time, most decided that it might be advisable to confront any problem areas themselves rather than waiting for the inspection team to do the job for them.

The adult educators, who had had genuine difficulty in knowing how to adapt their programme of courses to fit in with the funding conditions, took the requirement to carry out the self-assessment exercise as a direct attack on them and their work.

The head of department decided they neither had the time nor were willing to take part in the exercise. A meeting with the principal was demanded and granted.

It did not go well. The bursar had been invited to be present and that was seen as confrontational by the adult educators. Arguments developed and old grievances were aired.

The principal made the point that times had changed and that, like it or not, everyone had to examine past practices and look to the future. At this point, the discussions became even more acrimonious. The head of department said the principal should have fought the new regulations and not, as she put it, 'given in without demur'. She suggested that the new rules were no doubt what the principal wanted, namely to bring adult education into the examinations factory that the college had become.

At that stage, the principal lost patience. He asked what was wrong in accrediting courses or providing examination courses for any students who might want them, and insisted that quality assurance procedures should be devised. Two long serving members of staff countered by saying that it was obvious he had no understanding of their work; that accreditation and examinations were contrary to the principles embedded in non-vocational liberal adult education; that in any case no adult student would ever wish to take an examination; and that they had plenty of evidence of the quality of their provision. The fact that students returned year after year should, they said, be sufficient evidence of the quality of their provision. They accused the principal of challenging their professionalism and questioning their values. They complained that the culture of the college was anti-learning and that they would have none of it.

Stage 4: The bursar's revenge

The college bursar, weary of the arguing, and feeling strongly that the principal should have put an end to the arguments and just ordered them to do as they were told and to get on with it, presented information to the effect that student numbers had been falling for some years and that the age profile had risen. Adult education, he said, had become little more than a refuge for elderly people. By now warming to the attack, he added that he was confident that when the inspectors arrived, they would want to know what the department was doing to attract younger people. He claimed that the same courses had been provided year after year and he could see no signs of developmental work. Most damaging of all, he presented statistics which appeared to indicate that the college had been subsidizing the department for years and subsidies were no longer available. The college was already in danger of ending the year with a financial deficit and he promised he would do everything in his power to prevent it. His tone of voice was not conciliatory.

Stage 5: The move to improve

The adult educators were worried at the bursar's attitude. They had never regarded him as being supportive, but now they recognized they had an enemy in a key position. He had control of the money and would fight the principal and the governors if he thought their policies and actions were likely to cause problems. He had done it before, and won. Staff had to accept the bursar's evidence that numbers were falling and that the bursar was right about the age profile of the students. They had never compared numbers from one year to the next. They had never been asked to do that. They deplored, but understood the threats to their funding, but they did not know what to do. They spent many hours trying to produce a 'survival' paper, but could see no way of making changes to their normal practice.

They felt betrayed by the principal and his senior management team. The head of department felt confident that the college, with its large budget, could easily fund adult education, even if all government funding ceased for their work. Others, who began to feel that they had not been entirely fair in attacking the principal so forcibly, were less confident. They believed the bursar when he said no funding would be provided and felt that it would be wise to present a rather more positive front, show willing and just produce the required review in order to prove their quality. They argued that they should at least look again at the consultants' criticisms. When they had done that, they thought it might be possible to consider producing some sort of self-evaluation report.

Stage 6: The spring clean

It was eventually decided that an effort should be made to increase student numbers and to target younger age groups. An advertising campaign was planned, but the bursar, who was now focused on his prey, refused to authorize any funding. Leaflets were produced in the department and a door-to-door delivery was organized by a team of volunteers. The consultants had complained that the accommodation was shabby and that dustbins were kept by the front door. A volunteer group painted the common room. Dustbins were moved to the back of the building and other inexpensive and mainly cosmetic changes were introduced.

The head of department and her staff were at a loss to know what else they could do. They felt that it was not their fault if younger students did not wish to attend their classes. They could see no way in which their courses could be changed. They already worked long days, evenings and weekends – far in excess of contractual hours – and they felt they could do no more without more staff and more money. The principal made it clear they would get neither. He felt that he had given them every opportunity to provide him with a plan for survival, and a realistic self-assessment exercise with evidence to support what they claimed, but they seemed unable to look critically at their work, nor to understand that survival would depend on a fundamental change of approach.

Stage 7: The end of the line

The situation had become pressing and time had run out. The bursar felt closure was likely to be the only solution and that the problem had to be reported to the governors. The principal felt genuinely sorry at the prospect of closure of a department which provided a useful service for the community. He had spent a great deal of time with the adult educators when he first took up his post as principal, because he was aware of his lack of experience of their work. Staff had explained the principles involved in liberal non-vocational adult education as they saw it (their paradigm) and he understood clearly the depth of feeling for the retention of the paradigm at all costs. At the time, he felt that some of their assumptions were questionable, but as long as the department provided what members of the public appeared to want, and as long as there was funding, he had been willing to go along with them. Now, circumstances had changed and he regretted not having examined the assumptions more closely. What was worse, in spite of his efforts to take account of their views and to take a close interest in their work, he appeared to have failed to establish the kind of relationship with the adult educators which allowed rational discussion of perceived problems. Now it had to be over to the governors.

Stage 8: The governors' meeting

The discussion of the agenda item on the future of the department of adult education took more than an hour. Regrets were expressed at the seemingly inevitable closure of what had been a valuable community resource. However, several governors felt that the decision to close was too draconian and argued that one more attempt at restructuring should be made, subject to the members of the department being willing to meet three or four volunteer governors and to spend a day working out how the present difficulties might be resolved. When the offer of the staff–governors' meeting was presented to the adult educators, they complained that they were being asked to give up yet one more Saturday for nothing, but they had little choice but to agree.

Stage 9: The airing of values, beliefs and strengths

When danger of closure was first raised, and following the adverse consultants' report, the climate for change did not really exist among some of the adult educators, including their leader. In spite of all the evidence to the contrary, most did not really believe that their funding would disappear. They had done their best to become more efficient, had addressed almost all the consultants' complaints, and had worked until they were all exhausted. They felt that they could do no more. The Saturday meeting of governors and adult educators was clearly going to be the last desperate effort to save the department and at least some of the programme.

The three volunteer governors had had an earlier meeting to decide how they might structure the day and to appoint a chairman. They were anxious that the day did not degenerate into a complaints session. After some discussion, and in an effort to be positive, they decided that the adult educators should be asked to spend an hour writing down what they considered to be their strengths, not weaknesses, and to try to list what values and beliefs they held about adult education as provided in their department.

On the day, it took staff an hour to produce the following rough-and-ready list:

1 We provide a welcoming environment in which adults (admittedly mostly women over retirement age) can acquire skills and/or knowledge in a range of subjects.
2 Student satisfaction is paramount.
3 Quality of what is provided is decided by the students.
4 We believe our tutors are good and know their job.
5 We believe few (if any) adult students want accreditation for the work they do.
6 Tutor loyalty is important.
7 We believe the introduction of vocational work would impair the quality of our provision.
8 The content and methods of delivery of all courses should be decided by the students.
9 We provide classes which our students want, not what we want them to have.
10 We should not sit in judgement of our peers and so we should not embarrass our tutors by inspecting the way they teach. Tutors know their subject.
11 Students would not continue to attend if they were not satisfied.
12 We have an obligation to provide classes for disadvantaged students and they should be asked to pay only a nominal amount for their courses, or nothing at all. This is their right.
13 Retired students should also be asked to pay only a nominal amount for their courses. They have paid taxes and they are entitled to enjoy courses at little cost.

14 We consider tutors' ability to relate to adult students is even more important than qualifications.
15 The centre provides a lifeline for older people who live on the nearby run-down housing estate and it is important that this lifeline is not broken.
16 The centre is run on democratic lines. That is what makes adult education different from work done in the rest of the college.

Staff were anxious to inform governors about the efforts they had made to improve recruitment, the overtime they had willingly done and what they saw as the lack of support they had received from college managers. Their commitment to providing what they believed the public wanted and their belief in the right of individuals to have access to adult education were clear. Yet it seemed to the governors that the list contained a number of questionable assumptions and that the strength of their commitment might in itself be an inhibiting factor. Their beliefs, values and assumptions were so embedded that it became clear that any radical change was likely to be difficult. The efforts of the adult educators to change in order to improve had been made on top of the long accepted way of operating.

In spite of threats of closure and demands for a new look at their approach, there had been no evidence of a shift in values, priorities or assumptions. The adult educators had become entrenched and, as Handy (1993: 346) reminds us, 'When one of our basic assumptions runs out of steam, there is no longer any confident basis for predicting the future'. They had certainly run out of steam, had closed their collective mind to any notion of a future different from anything they had known in the past and had allowed what Johnson (1992: 30) described as 'strategic drift' to take over. It was clear to the governors, though not to the adult educators at this stage, that a paradigm shift (Kuhn 1970: 89) was necessary if any progress was to be made.

Stage 10: The paradigm shift

Once the beliefs and assumptions had been aired, governors felt confident that it should become possible to discuss ways in which external influences had to be taken into account if the department were to survive, but this was hard for the staff to accept. It still constituted, in their view, a criticism of their values and a questioning of all their beliefs. Peters and Waterman (1982: 42) warned that 'after a paradigm shift begins, progress is fast though fraught with tension. People get angry'. And some of the adult educators did.

The governors, fast running out of goodwill, wisely decided it was time to call a halt to the discussions, but requested that the group should meet again once more in a week's time. They decided that if any progress were to be made, they (the governors) would need to do more work before the next meeting. They decided to look in more detail at the adult educators' list of strengths, beliefs and values, and to consider the influence of the assumptions implicit in the list. They spent as much time as they could afford talking to part-time tutors and students: they reviewed the criticisms of the management of the department in the consultants' report and then listed their findings, as follows, using headings devised by Johnson (1992: 28–36) in his study of approaches to strategy development in organizations.

Organization

- Little *formal* organization, as far as they could see.
- The head of department seen by some part-time tutors as autocratic.
- Decision making stated by the head of department as being through the Student Council, but the Student Council had not met for the past two years, and the programme had changed very little in the past three years.

Control systems

- None in place, as far as they could see.
- No quality assurance system, no budgeting, no mission statement or development plans. The head of department said none had ever been asked for until now.

Stories

- Satisfaction of students (but no evidence to demonstrate that that was so).

- How good things were in the old days when there was little hassle about money and when nobody interfered with what they were doing.
- Enemies in the college, who neither knew nor cared about educating adults.
- Other departments in the college got more consideration than adult education (though staff unable to demonstrate that that was true).

Rituals and routines

- All staff work long hours (appeared to be true that they worked long hours, but it was not clear where the time went).
- Tutors quickly learnt 'how things were done around here' and conformed.
- Belief that students did not want classes in the mornings or out of term time (but no evidence that attempts had been made to find out).
- Enrolment always on one day and one evening in September, the week before classes started. It had always been like that (but no evidence that that was the most efficient way of enrolling students, nor that that was what students wanted).
- Classes organized on the basis of what 'went' last year. If they 'went' last year, that was considered to be proof that the courses were good and that they were what students wanted.

Symbols

- Office with the head of department's name, qualifications and 'No access to students' sign on the door. No doubt who was the boss.
- Coffee brought to her every morning by the cleaner. 'Real' coffee served in nice china. Cleaner washed the china. This proved to be a major cause of irritation to members of staff, who had to queue in the canteen for what they described as a choice between coffee made out of acorns or stewed tea served in plastic cups.

Stage 11: Crisis time

At the next meeting of the governors and adult educators, the list was presented. The head of department contested many of the statements. She said that it was insulting to suggest that there was little formal organization, and she was certainly not autocratic. She demanded to know who had said she was autocratic. She firmly believed in democratic management. It was not her fault that the Student Council had not met for two years. If students did not want to attend, that was up to them. She did not believe 'control' had any place in adult education, and the quality assurance system being introduced into the college was not suitable for their work. Standards were not good, she said, in some other departments of the college, yet people were willing to criticize adult education because they did not make money. She asked, 'Are we going to have to produce balance sheets to demonstrate we are doing a good job?' She felt that governors were like the principal. They were criticizing the work but they understood nothing of the values of adult education.

Stage 12: High noon

Crisis time had arrived. One of the governors said that a decision had to be made. They had all given up two Saturdays and got nowhere. He suggested everyone went away for an hour to cool down and reconsider their approach. Anyone willing to start discussions again would reconvene, but only if they were prepared to come with an open mind, were prepared to consider the implications of some of the present difficulties, and to see if there were any ways in which a paradigm shift could be achieved without destroying the best of what had been achieved in the past.

An hour later, the group did convene, but without three of the adult educators and one governor. Then, work began in earnest. The adult educators who returned spoke frankly, and in some sadness, that their present practices were being challenged but in the hour of heart searching which had taken place, they had begun to accept that changes had to be made. There was some serious discussion as to whether an accredited course might, just conceivably, be able to maintain the best of liberal adult education. Writing down 'the way we do things here' had clarified the situation, but at a cost to some of the individuals concerned. In the end, it was accepted that the paradigm might have dominated the development of a more dynamic department and possibly had caused resistance to change. After all the hours of talking and arguing, a small but significant step forward had been taken.

Stage 13: The move to the new-look department

All change is threatening. The hard lesson learnt, at least by some of the participants, was that no approach can remain static. Values and assumptions will need to be questioned from time to time and adjustments made to take account of new findings, new demands and new circumstances, but that is not to say that every principle, every value and belief has to be thrown away in the process.

This was the position to which the adult educators held fast. A great deal of good work had in fact been done in the department and they were determined it should not be lost.

Not everyone felt able to cope with the changes and two members of staff, including the head of department, requested and were granted early retirement. The remaining members of staff took stock, and gradually, a draft development plan was devised and a new style programme planned and launched. The first year of the new programme of mainly accredited courses, student numbers fell dramatically, as staff said they would, but gradually, new students began to register for courses and numbers of regular attenders began to return. It was clear that things would never be the same again.

Not an unqualified success story, but at least the department was saved, though with a very different structure. Staff learnt new skills, became adept at obtaining funding for special purposes, and even the bursar expressed a degree of approval at the way things were shaping up and the way staff had, as he put it, 'faced up to reality'.

Postscript

The conflicts had raised a number of issues which had college-wide implications. The principal thought he had established a good relationship with the staff of the department. He felt that he had done his best to consult, to support and to understand their concerns. Reflecting on what had happened, he said,

> Now, I think I agree with the bursar that I went wrong by allowing the discussions to go on for too long and to reach the stage of personal abuse. We were in the middle of a crisis and time was against us. I should have said, 'Look here. You know what the position is. You have all the facts. It's a case of change or perish. I may not like it any more than you do, but

WE HAVE NO CHOICE. Let's try to salvage the best of what we have or else we are in danger of losing the lot.' They presented me with a stone wall. They were not about to move from their original position. What do you do then?

There's a limit to the time that can be spent consulting, listening to objections but deciding nothing. They wanted me to wave my magic wand and to say 'It's all right. Don't worry. The way you are doing things is the best, so we'll just write to the funding body and say we don't want to join. Just keep giving us the money though.' Well, I couldn't.

The bursar, who never minces his words, told me afterwards I had caused some of the problems myself because when I arrived I visited all the departments and appeared to be commending them all for their splendid work, regardless of whether they deserved it or not. That gave them all confidence that their way of operating was first class, when in some cases it was a very long way from being excellent. He may have been right. I had certainly and, with hindsight unwisely, accepted departments' claims that they were very successful and ran good quality courses. The adult educators regularly spoke about their values and their commitment to students. It all sounded worthy. I had not asked for evidence of what students were actually learning and because they had few accredited courses, they were not subject to the controls in place in other departments, most of which I have to say were imposed by the various validating and examining bodies rather than by the college.

With a certain amount of irritation, he continued

Some people in this college are still living in the good old days when there was enough money and nobody really had to be accountable, apart from ensuring that the exam results were OK and nobody ran off with college funds.

It's all very well people who write books and have never had to face the problems of managing fundamental change in large institutions telling us to take account of individual differences and to respect the value priorities of all and sundry, but what if those value priorities don't make any sense? What then? Just tell me how. I'm willing to learn. If you can find me a quick-and-easy solution, I shall be pleased to hear it.

A year later, no 'quick-and-easy solutions' had emerged, mainly because, as Harvey-Jones (1988: 1) pointed out, there is no such thing as 'the instant prescription, which if followed will solve every ill from bankruptcy to athlete's foot'. However, writing about the lessons he learnt in his career as a manager, Harvey-Jones continued:

> What there has been is a steady process of learning that management and business is a pragmatic matter depending entirely on people and how they react. Everything I have learnt teaches me that it is only when you work with rather than against people that achievement and lasting success is possible.
>
> (Harvey-Jones 1988: 1)

The principal agreed with those sentiments, in principle, but had found the practice hard to achieve. As he pointed out, there will always be a gap between theories and what Møller (1996: 101) described as 'theories-in-use'. People react in different ways to different situations, and somehow, ways have to be found of dealing with issues involving fundamental change without destroying the individuals involved.

Commentary

The stages of challenge, resistance, breakdown of relationships, crisis and imposed changes of practice are certainly not unique to this one institution. We have heard similar accounts of situations in schools, in other colleges and in universities – and not only in the UK. The literature relating to the management of change and coping in times of crisis is now extensive. It is always easy to describe what went wrong after the event, to point to unwise approaches, to condemn certain practices and to sneer at 'crisis management', but life has changed dramatically in education and the large number of early retirement applications from senior managers in all sectors of education should tell us something about the strains of life at the top.

In a climate of frequent changes in policy and funding, demands to do more (and better) on less, to produce new courses at short notice, often without having the time to evaluate what has gone before; in such a climate, it is easy to see how decisions can sometimes be made on expediency rather than on educational grounds. Survival is, after all, rather important to all concerned, in education and in the business world.

There are differences between business and education though, one of which is that in education we were always accustomed to a large degree of personal and professional autonomy. The rule of the educational world was that we knew best and so would brook no interference from outsiders. That autonomy is now challenged and our territory is being invaded, but individuals working in a 'first among equals' environment are unlikely to touch their caps and agree to whatever their managers rule, if they have no understanding of why a particular line is being taken. Complaints about managers keeping essential information to themselves are common enough, but keeping secrets and claiming that certain information is too confidential to make public can prove counterproductive.

Ed Carlson, former president of United Airlines, once said, 'Nothing is worse for morale than a lack of information down in the ranks. I call it NETMA – Nobody Ever Tells Me Anything – and I have tried hard to minimize that problem' (reported in Peters and Waterman 1982: 267).

The case study principal was committed to the view that there should be no secrets in his college and that staff should be made aware of circulars and policy statements from government and professional organizations. However, effective communication is difficult to achieve in large organizations and even with e-mail or, as some users maintain, because of e-mail, there is serious information overload, as is demonstrated in Chapter 3. The college has still not resolved the problem of how to keep everyone informed about policy changes without distributing so much material that no one reads anything, including important items, but it is certainly aware of the importance of making information available and is making efforts to improve.

Important though the sharing of information is, it should come as no surprise to anyone that individuals who find themselves under attack will fight their corner, as happened in the case of the adult educators. Once territory and autonomy is threatened, then interest sets are formed, loyalty relates only to the area being challenged, battle lines are drawn and minds are closed to any notion of cooperation, collaboration or change. We become tiresome, devious and aggressive. Micropolitics takes over (Ball 1987: ch. 2; Hoyle 1982: 87–98, 1986: 51–7).

The adult educators fought hard for the continuation of the way they had always done things and throughout the negotiations never felt it necessary to question their own position. They had seen the documentation relating to changes in funding, but their perception that they were right and the principal was wrong blinded them to consideration of any alternative. Perhaps the environment and ethos of the college did not encourage consideration of alternatives. The principal, on reflection, accepted that the adult educators might not have had the opportunity to grow, to be involved in cross-college working groups, to understand cross-specialism working practices and so to understand the points of view of staff in other subject areas. The department had been a free-standing adult centre, funded by the local education authority, before it was 'taken over' by the college. Perhaps insufficient effort had been made to enable the staff to integrate into college life and to develop a sense of college in addition to departmental loyalty. Even so, the principal was in no frame of mind to accept total responsibility for the adult educators' isolation from college life. He made it clear that they should have made efforts to learn, understand and take advantage of what the college provided in the way of training and development, for the sake of their own professionalism, rather than blaming college management for everything. Nevertheless steps were taken to ensure that in future they participated fully in all college meetings and activities and the new head of department was automatically included in the college 'managing a department' seminars.

It was found that some of the staff grievances were justified. They were located in premises a mile from the main campus. In spite of repeated requests, they were still not on the college internal telephone system. They were not on e-mail, as everyone else was. It was discovered that they did not always receive notices of important meetings and so did not attend. How could they?

They had had no base in the main building and were not allocated parking permits. As a result, when they visited the college, they had to fight for a parking space – and so they preferred not to go. The college administrators had been aware of those problems for some time, but had always claimed that the funds were not available to upgrade the adult education facilities. Space for parking on the main campus was limited and in their view, it was just not reasonable to be asked to keep slots empty on the offchance that one or more of the adult educators might wish to 'drop in' some time. The college had plans to build a new block on the main campus eventually, and the expenditure involved in upgrading systems in the department of adult education was not considered to be justified. However, it was discovered that the optimistic estimate for the completion of the new block was in the region of ten years, and ten years is a very long time in the life of a department. The crisis brought the grievances to the fore again and steps were taken to implement a staged programme of updating and refurbishing.

It is possible that some of the changes, several of which resulted in a marked improvement in staff morale, would have taken place regardless of the events leading up to the restructuring of the department of adult education. However, it seems certain that the changes were accelerated as a result of the experience gained over that traumatic period.

The principal's final word on the outcome of the case study was:

Change is inevitable and we have to face that. If we don't go forward, we go backwards. We are overtaken by our competitors. I don't like what is happening in education now any more than a good many others in the college, but we can't keep arguing and grumbling about things we can't alter.

I feel very strongly that it's not my exclusive responsibility to manage change. Everyone in the organization has to be prepared to understand and, if necessary, give way on some issues in the interests of the college and the students who depend on us to give them the best learning experiences possible. That will always be hard and I'm not so naive as to think there won't be more battles ahead. But I do hope some people will realise that I'm not a genius. There's a limit to what I can achieve without their involvement and support. I'm trying, but I need help.

Perhaps the college should be grateful it has a principal who readily admits he is not a genius. As Drucker (1977: 361) reminds us, 'No organization can depend on genius: the supply is always scarce and unreliable'. And the last thing an educational institution needs is an unreliable leader!

3

ARE YOU REALLY *HEARING* THIS? COMMUNICATING FOR QUALITY LEARNING

A speaker: There are about five thousand languages on earth,
and we can't find one that we both understand!
A listener: What on earth are you talking about?

(Maloney 1996: 26)

The arts of evading communication are, as Maloney implies, just
as extensive as the means by which we communicate. The conflict
of values studied in Chapter 2 was caused, in part, by failures of
communication within the college. Where schools and colleges
are concerned, many different kinds of people – with diverse backgrounds, language, culture, interests and ambitions – can be thrown
together in one artificial setting. This casual conglomeration has
sometimes produced explosive mixtures for schools in urban settings, even though both staff and students can retreat into their own
communities after school hours. When, however, the school is itself
in a remote setting, then it may become a place where the quality
of learning inevitably depends on the quality of communication.

This chapter draws on visits made to schools in remote parts of
the mid-west region in Western Australia where, for reasons that

will become clear, the quality of communication both within and beyond the school can never be taken for granted. The visits were arranged as part of the first phase in a large collaborative research project carried out by staff of a university faculty of education (Harrison *et al.* 1997), to determine patterns of retention, motivation and achievement among Aboriginal school students. The project aimed to identify, through observation and consultations with schools and their communities, significant examples of good policies, practice and team building in this crucial area of provision for Aboriginal and Torres Strait Islander people.

The main focus for this chapter is on the daily operations of three school principals and their staff, who work in community or high schools in the remote mid-west region. Each school has its own unique setting, yet the schools share similar conditions through their remoteness. Of particular importance was the fact that the teaching staff could not avoid being significant presences in the local community, both within and outside usual school hours. 'We are *never* not on duty', as one teacher put it. In these conditions, the quality of interpersonal relations and, specifically, of managing these, can swiftly improve or swiftly harm the learning climate in a school and – with more dramatic inevitability than in the city – in a remote, dispersed community. The power of the principal, individual teachers and teacher teams to do good or damage is greatly magnified.

Some months before these visits took place, there had been an 'incident' involving school staff and the community, where the direct cause had been a not unfamiliar confrontation between a member of the community and inexperienced school staff. An angry parent had made a threatening remark in the school, during school hours. The school reverted to the rule book (rather than to common sense) and sent her off the premises. When she returned with some equally angry community friends, the school staff walked out; TV and press media became involved, and an event that had begun with just one disgruntled parent who had acted inappropriately, ended as an incident where control had to be taken beyond the hands of the school staff. Some important lessons emerged, in particular about the need for constant, honest dialogue among school staff and the community, so that problems might be addressed before they became too large to handle by those who are directly involved. Although a School Community Council had been in place as required by the education authority, the school needed to develop more 'on the spot' systems to handle individual difficulties as they arose, and to achieve the high levels of school–community communication on which good social order, let alone good academic progress, depended.

The actual scale of 'remote and rural' contexts in Western Australia may be ascertained on the 'radio map' (Figure 3.1). The Meekatharra School of the Air has been established since the 1930s in the region to serve the children of pastoralists in outlying farms (who often farm on what would be huge acreages in European terms) and who have no road access to the few schools in the region. The School of the Air serves students of school age whose homes are so isolated that they are out of reach of even the most remote schools or settlements. Meekatharra is itself a small remote mining town, 800 kilometres north-east of Perth, where the School of the Air is established on the site of the high school. Other townships (small villages) are indicated in capital letters on the map, and each of these has a community or high school. They are accessible, either by road or dirt track. The names that are not in capital letters are not accessible by road (see Figure 3.1).

Confronting 'adaptive challenges'

Principals and their teaching staff in these remote schools cannot escape being in the first line of confronting what Heifetz and Laurie (1997: 124) have called 'adaptive challenges'. They suggest that 'adaptive work is required when our deeply held beliefs are challenged, when the values that make us successful become less relevant, and when legitimate, yet competing perspectives emerge'. Unlike the situation confronting the adult educators in Chapter 2, the main challenge to teachers in these schools lay in the fact that the pupils and the communities which the schools served were themselves faced with continuous adaptive challenge. Although the remote contexts of these schools may suggest a never changing rural idyll, in fact, they experience dynamic change forces even more acutely than do city based schools. The catching up that must be achieved in such settings, to ensure that students and their communities have similar educational, social and work opportunities to those who live in the cities, cannot help but be disruptive, if it is to be effective.

Heifetz and Laurie identified six principles for meeting adaptive challenge: all of these have significant application to the huge communicative adaptations that each of the three school principals

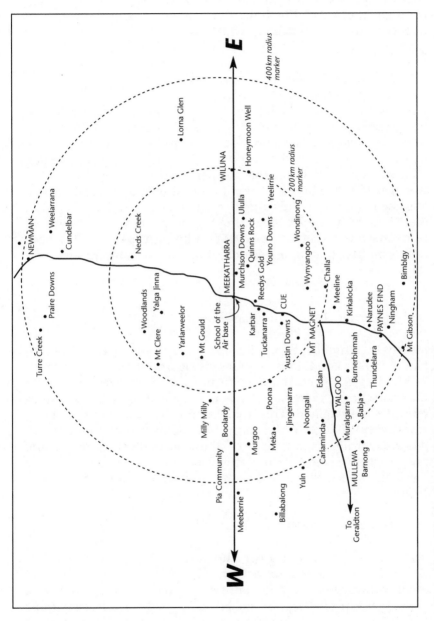

Figure 3.1 Meekatharra School of the Air

and their teaching staff had to make. We have used these six principles (with our own comments added) to show how, in certain
contexts, they can all be important components in the major art
of successful communication with people.

Getting on the balcony

Getting on the balcony, or being able to stand back, while also
being engaged in operations, might almost seem like the art of developing *non*-communication, since it underlines self-possession
and independence, and a willingness to withdraw from the permanent shoulder rubbing that happens in any busy school. Given
the insulated conditions of teaching in a remote or rural setting,
and the importance of making oneself open and available, it is not
easy to develop the art of 'getting on the balcony'. Yet, as will be
seen, ingenious solutions were found by principals and teachers,
to ensure that they took personal time out to think through critical issues.

Identifying the adaptive challenge

Identifying the adaptive challenge, or developing prescience in
handling new conditions, requires giving priority to creating trust,
in building a shared response to unusual challenges. In remote
or rural schools, exemplary levels of consultation with local communities are required. This involves, for example, never meeting
expressions of anger with returns of anger, whether personally or
bureaucratically expressed; not falling into the trap of playing
unconstructive games such as might be expected of 'uncaring city
dwellers', who represent a distant, uninformed 'authority'.

Regulating distress

Regulating distress, or creating a holding environment, means that
all concerned can rely on a framework of shared decencies and
order, within which disputes are settled. Heifetz and Laurie (1997:
128) regard 'regulating distress' as being 'perhaps a leader's most
difficult job'. As well as creating a holding environment, important
aspects of regulating distress include directing, protecting, managing

conflict and shaping norms. It involves projecting a personal 'presence and poise' (p. 128) when under stress. Successful experts in this area have an unusual emotional capacity to tolerate uncertainty, frustration and pain. The principals and staff of the three schools visited did well in these important aspects, though as will be seen, this was achieved at more cost to some than to others.

Maintaining disciplined attention

Maintaining disciplined attention is considered to be the hard 'currency' of leadership (Heifetz and Laurie 1997: 129). It is an essential aspect of good communication to be willing to do even more than listen to the discourse of others. Disciplined attention requires listeners to be able to say 'I *hear* you'; that is, I read or understand what you are saying, and also why you need to say it. Thorough listening leads, for example, to deepening discussions, through asking well targeted questions; it involves a reluctance to blame outside circumstances; it is matched by a concern to develop a sense of personal and shared responsibility, to take events forward. Where there is a sincere interest in getting teams to 'listen and learn from each other – the principal or team leader can get conflict out into the open and use it as a source of creativity' (Jan Carlzon, quoted in Heifetz and Laurie 1997: 128). Any kind of conflict has potential dangers, especially in remote settings; yet the principals in the schools and numerous staff members showed how candour in facing critical issues and points of behaviour can serve as an excellent survival device on behalf of all parties concerned.

Giving the work back to the people

Giving the work back to the people means providing support for, not control over, staff. Good principals and team leaders are delighted when individuals and teams take initiatives. Just as classroom learners may lapse all too early into passive compliance, rote learning and the like, so may a teaching staff take the easy route of doing no more than what they are told, and shift into 'habits of work avoidance, that shield people from responsibility, pain and the need to change' (Heifetz and Laurie 1997: 129). Giving the work back to people is the only way to generate 'collective self-confidence' throughout the school. And, as will be seen in the study that follows, self-confidence among the staff generates self-confidence among classroom learners.

Protecting voices of leadership from below

Protecting voices of leadership from below is important because, along with owning the work, people also need their own voices, both individual and collective. A remarkable feature of the visits to these three schools was the constructive forthrightness with which even the most recently qualified teachers discussed issues such as their own recent experiences as trainee teachers, and the problems that they had found during the first few months in demanding new posts. Their criticisms were, typically, calm and authoritative and, with one exception, betrayed no feelings of resentment in having to cope with unusual and difficult challenges. Following one or two informal conversations with the new teachers, it was clear that what they had to say was of such interest that it was worth conducting more formal interviews with them. As a result, much useful advice, based on their experience, both as teachers and as new postholders, was communicated back to the university faculty of education which has a major role in the provision of initial teacher education. Some details of these are provided in the accounts to follow. A key difference emerges in this sixth principle, between the principal's or team leader's authority, which authorizes others to act, as opposed to authoritarianism, which inhibits them, until they are told what to do. When the 'voices from below' are speaking up, then 'the people who needed to do the changing here finally framed the adaptive challenge for themselves' (Heifetz and Laurie 1997: 132). Enough had been changed among the teaching staff in these three schools, to hope that the same message had also spread throughout the school to all its learners and, throughout the community to all parents and others involved.

The schools

The singular self-containment of the schools and their communities provides 'laboratory' conditions, where the varying impact of interpersonal relations can be readily recorded. However, even in these settings, there is a considerable interdependence among the schools themselves, as well as central links with the State Education

Department. The school principals were the main (but not sole) agents in maintaining inter-school networks. 'The centre' provided input through the services of an experienced 'hands on' district superintendent who made regular visits and engaged in full consultations with each school. Moreover, the director-general of the State Education Department had visited each of the three schools a few days before our own visit. Both the interdependent links and the main link with the centre are significant factors for ensuring that, for example, an exciting initiative in one school does not degenerate into a merely eccentric departure from the group norm, but is recognized by others as a genuine educational innovation.

School A

This is classified as a remote community school and is the most remote of the three schools. It is in a small former goldmining township with a population of about 250 people (formerly around 9000 at the height of its goldmining activities in the 1920s). It is situated on the great plateau of Western Australia about 1000 kilometres north-east of Perth. The township is on a granite rise, and adjoins a large, shallow lake. The landscape is a wilderness, with a wide distribution of pre-Cambrian rocks in the region, where only scrub and vegetation thrive; it is a stark landscape, which endures long periods of aridity, and extreme variations of temperature. The township is settled by the Aboriginal Wongi people and by non-settler non-Aboriginal groups, who have access to a virtually unlimited water supply from surrounding shallow lakes. Each spring brings a stunning abundance of wildflowers, providing more evidence of contradiction and contrast in the living conditions of the region.

The school is reached by driving down 200 kilometres of dirt road; drivers are advised to take two good spare tyres for the journey. Visitors are warned in the School Information Guide that 'white clothes don't stay white for long here'. There are four class groups in the school, for Years 1/2, 3/4, 5/6/7 (ages 5 to 12 years) and secondary; the school has a principal, a registrar, five teachers of Aboriginal descent, one Aboriginal teacher and four Aboriginal support staff. Classrooms live up to the standards policy of the school, which states that 'a bright, colourful, stimulating and tidy classroom is an ideal environment for children to learn in'. Other school documentation includes an accountability document, which advises teaching staff on a range of accountability issues, including performance indicators for curriculum and other areas; an information guide; numerous documents on aspects of literacy, numeracy and teaching multi-grade and transferable skills; and extensive advice on staff dynamics, which addresses issues of communication throughout the school. Staff dynamics is taken seriously, both in the documentation and in daily organization of the school:

> In a school such as this, the staff tends to work closely together, and they also live and socialize together. Living and working together in an isolated and difficult environment can lead to a build up of tensions, and can cause staff problems. There are many contributing factors to these tensions. These may include: missing family and friends; relations changing over time; perceived differences in workloads; differing religious, political or social views; differences in personal interests and habits; differing standards of tidiness; pressures of a new job; reaction to isolation; a feeling of no real privacy. Problems can often be exacerbated by factors such as intolerance, outside interference, lack of communication and lack of understanding.
>
> Extreme examples of breakdowns in relationships can see people not talking and not co-operating at home, and not talking and not co-operating at school. Often others can become involved, and school morale can be affected. It can become obvious to the community that the school is having problems and this can affect the standing of the school in the community.
>
> (Staff Dynamics Guide)

The document then goes on to address ways in which new staff might be able to resolve such problems. Following this catalogue of unusual challenges for new staff (how many schools need to include a list such as this, as essential early reading for new staff?), the document provides guidelines for preventing such problems. These include basic rules such as ensuring that school and domestic duties are fairly shared, and there is frequent reference to the need for respect, consideration, flexibility, tolerance and sharing of problems. More, perhaps, than any other document that the school has prepared, this Staff Dynamics Guide reveals just what new teaching staff might really expect, and what is expected of them, in schools that serve remote communities.

One further important point about this school, with its 85 per cent Aboriginal student population, is the considerable efforts made by the schools to achieve effective policies for improving the health of students. This includes a health bus which makes regular visits; health checks; provision of showers for students on the school premises; availability of cooked meals; a uniform pool of clean clothes; and clear attainment targets and indicators for continuous improvement in this area. The efforts made by the school to develop good community links have included local employers; as a result of patient negotiations, local mining companies have confirmed that they are willing to offer real jobs to Year 10 school leavers.

School B

This district high school is classed as rural, rather than remote. Yet it is 900 kilometres north-east of Perth, in a small township which has grown as a ribbon development along a main road in the region. It is twice as large as School A, and about half of the students are of Aboriginal descent. Its advantage in terms of size and location is noted at once by visitors to the reception area of the school. This is newly furbished, welcoming, and proclaims both efficiency and openness to all who come to the school. The school documentation for staff is, again, extensive, and rather more rules based than advice based, which was the case of School A. This includes systematic advice, for example, on Managing Student Behaviour and on Aboriginal Education Strategies. This latter document acknowledges that classes in the school 'are generally taught by non-Aboriginal teachers who have had little or no experience with Aboriginal people'. Although it accepts that there are no prescribed 'correct' strategies here, it offers much constructive advice, some general (for example, students '*can* learn given correct strategies, environment and curriculum') and some particular (for example, in developing positive attitudes, 'recognize that some traditional concepts still maintain a very strong influence on contemporary culture'; that is, many students in this school will have a mix of cultural influences that is considerably more complex than may be the case with their teachers). The latest School Development Plan, which is updated each year, addresses 'behaviour management priorities'; it lists phases of performance management, from programme indicators through data collection, strategies, resources, timelines (scheduling) and costs. There is a high priority given to health care (second only to behaviour management), which (as in School A) aims to reduce the incidence of problems associated with such common problems among the student community as personal hygiene, nutrition, and ear care (since middle ear disease is a common affliction among Aboriginal communities).

School C

This is also a district high school, which is located in a small mining township about 600 kilometres north-east of Perth. A well written, attractively presented School Development Plan document provides extensive information about the school. With about 150 school students, from pre-primary years to Year 10 and fourteen teaching staff, it is larger than School A and smaller than School B. There are some students in Years 11 and 12, who are completing a pre-vocational course for entry into further education, through the Distance Education Centre of the school, which links with larger cities in the State. The township is sited within the traditional lands of the Budimaya Aboriginal people, and two-fifths of student population are of Aboriginal descent. Over one-third of the families in the township are dependent on welfare benefits. The school buildings are composed entirely of transportable units, although a new permanent administration centre and staff room were under construction at the time of our visit. The school manages to provide a balanced and comprehensive curriculum, with a strong emphasis on language and numeracy skills, and with ambitious standards identified in these areas. The school also provides a range of special learning programmes. These include: Aboriginal languages (in partnership with the Aboriginal community); Japanese (via computer based technology); fire and rescue cadets (in partnership with the town's volunteer fire brigade); specialized physical education and outdoor education; and mining traineeships (in partnership with local industry and a regional further education college). The school has allocated two teachers (or a teacher with support teacher) for all language lessons, in order to provide small group and individualized learning. There is also a full-time Aboriginal education worker whose task is to strengthen and extend community liaison. A further distinctive feature of this school is the establishment of a comprehensive computer network which provides network services to each classroom, inclusive of educational learning packages, CD-ROM library and e-mail.

As with Schools A and B, the classrooms in School C were inviting, full of bright displays of work, and there was a pleasant and orderly working climate throughout the school. Performance targets and indicators were specified for each of the main curriculum areas. There were also specific targets for buildings and environment; staffing quality, and school management, with three year phases of development in each of these areas. Non-curriculum priorities included information skills for students; social skills; health; attendance rates, and community perceptions of the school. However, the school faced considerable problems in collecting appropriate data for monitoring these targets. In English, for example, 'as the school has a highly transient student population, the aggregate data of the school is a poor indicator of the progress of the school in this priority area' (School Development Plan). The solution proposed by the school to this was to 'monitor key students who have been attending the school for a period of time'. The school documentation included frank discussion of such problems. It was also notably positive in tone. For example, it emphasized that 'parents are welcome to the school. Children need to know that their parents are interested in education'; and, on discipline, 'the school ensures that all students learn in an environment free from the destruction of others'.

The people who run the schools

If we wish to enhance teachers' professional lives, we have to direct our inquisitive gaze at teachers' own experienced worlds, and from there, pose demanding questions to those who seek to change and restructure the teacher's work from above. For at the end of the day, teacher professionalism is what teachers and others experience it as being, not what policy-makers and others assert it should become. The experience of professionalism and of its denial are to be found by studying the everyday work of teaching.

(Hargreaves and Goodson 1995: 22–3)

Hargreaves and Goodson are right to underline that it is what teachers are actually doing in schools, that constitutes professionalism. However, the 'experience of professionalism and its denial' is also evident throughout the networks that influence particular schools. The personal impact of a highly committed and energetic district superintendent could be seen through the even handed attention that was given in all three schools to such areas as school development planning, monitoring and accountability processes. He encouraged school principals to systematically engage staff in the exercise of self-evaluation, and of improving and reporting on schools' performance. Yet this superintendent was also convinced that no principal could achieve excellence in these challenging settings, merely by following the State Education Department's rule books and guidelines. In fact, he showed considerable interest in the individual stamp that particular principals and their staff were able to put on a school. He predicted, for example, that our reception at School A would be unconventional, as indeed it was. Having travelled 200 kilometres down a dust track where kangaroos, emus and eagles were out in force, following rains and the approach of dusk, we were invited into the principal's home. We were soon drinking homemade beer, sitting on comfortable chairs among piles of books and papers and sharing discussion with his partner (the school's registrar) and several of the staff. The evening meal, shared with the staff, was a blend of lighthearted banter and anecdote with serious and sometimes deep discussion about staff experiences in the schools. The principal could move easily from teasing one of the visitors about his headgear (an unremarkable blue cap) into careful listening and tactful counselling on behalf of one of the young staff, who had encountered a difficult incident during that afternoon at the school.

The school bus

As was the case with the other two schools, the principal took personal charge of the school bus, which toured homes and hamlets within a radius of 10–15 kilometres of the school. This was an important opportunity for the principals to talk to parents in the community, and to share talk with children in the bus. By driving the bus themselves, the principals enacted their message about the importance of school attendance. While we were travelling, Principal A commented on the need for a common, continuous curriculum that would operate in all schools of his kind, to meet the needs of wandering communities. Although a State curriculum was being devised for imminent introduction into schools, it was more a matter of remote and rural schools consulting and agreeing on some broad approaches for each term (for example, an agreement that during a particular set of weeks, specific aspects of mathematics or reading development could be handled). This was a good example (and was matched by further examples from the other two principals) of the advice from Heifetz and Laurie (1997: 125) to 'get on the balcony above the field of play', in order to reflect on the larger patterns of play that the school is engaged in.

It became clear, while driving around on these school bus trips, that in an important sense, these schools are no more remote than, for example, some schools that are trapped in ghettoes of social deprivation in parts of the UK. These remote and rural schools were addressing, much more self-consciously than might otherwise be the case, issues of communication and the dangers of noncommunication. There was little sense that isolation was causing great professional problems for the teachers. The visit to these rural Aboriginal communities was important, in that it revealed how many of the students exist in, to quote the principal of School A, 'third world conditions'. He emphasized that, while many problems are complex and not easily solved, many things can be put right by straightforward policies, including getting around to families and collecting children to ensure good attendance at the school. Parents want their children to be able to read, write and use number – just as children in the cities. As with the other principals, he was a great believer in identifying and pursuing standards and benchmarks. Schools not only must be seen in their own context, but also needed to work within an identified framework.

The principal had strong views on the curriculum being at the centre of successful policies on behalf of the students in his school. He discussed the plurality of influences on the children in the school, which include television and video, and other chance influences from outside traditional cultural patterns (e.g. advertising). One of his reasons for inviting the director-general of the State Education Department to the area was to draw attention to some problems both in his own and other schools in the district. These included issues of staff houses, housing maintenance and transfer of staff. As had been witnessed during the meal, both he and his partner, as registrar, were frequently preoccupied by ensuring that there is motivation and remotivation of usually transient younger staff.

The prominent availability of showers in the school, the medical bus, and full personal facilities, including meals, raise the need to redefine 'paternalism'. The provision of ordinary domestic decencies gives this school a most important family role, without which it would be able to do its job much less effectively. The good spirit of self-help characterizing domestic arrangements in the school extended also to systematic planning and evaluation for continuous school improvement. All three principals (but especially in Schools A and C) were genuinely interested in research and academic development as a crucial aspect of their own professional development. They were all pursuing advanced studies, in one case up to doctoral level, and had good ideas about the kinds of research which were likely to be both interesting and useful, not only for their own schools but also for other areas of education. For example, combination classes which sometimes involved two or even three year groups were common in their schools. Economics of class sizes required this, although it would be a dubious practice to defend in an affluent city suburban school. Mason and Burns (1997: 48–9) claim that studies of combination classes 'should investigate parents' and students' views of combination classes, as the literature is silent on how they perceive and think about these classes'. Yet all the principals revealed that they had shared their own strong curiosities about progress in such classes with students, staff and also parents.

Continuous shared discourse

Such continuous shared discourse, on important issues which included handling of the curriculum, performance management, school attendance and staffing issues, was taken for granted. All the principals were concerned that programmes such as the Aboriginal Support for Parents programme should be genuinely functional and lead to strong team action. This applied to other schemes, such as the community development employment programme, which allowed the schools to employ people, who would otherwise be out of work, for the benefit of the school. The principals promoted the views of the superintendent, that there must be several kinds of networking throughout the school and community, which can then feed into a common pool through the various conduits, for example, consultations with local community leaders; consultations with individual parents; sausage-sizzler events; open days; ensuring that when students are troubled they have immediate opportunities to talk about good and bad aspects of their day. Principal A stressed the importance of being able to produce student books to parents, which he considered to be much more important than end-of-semester reports. The link with the local police sergeant was also important in the schools, as was the direct relation that the principals had with the community leader.

In the view of Principal A, regular scheduled meetings with members of the School Council were less useful in attracting the community than showing that he and the staff were willing to deal with issues as they arose. He gave an example of averting the kind of crisis which has a chance of developing on any given day: a parent who was noisily and aggressively haranguing staff, to a point where he was tempted to call in the police. Instead he invited a grandparent to mediate, let her daughter talk through her anger and gradually distance the row that had been going on, away from the classroom area of the school. It transpired that the daughter had been evicted that morning from her home and, understandably, was inclined to blame all non-Aboriginal agencies for what, in her view, was a deeply unfair act against her and her family. In a community which suffers considerable problems of unemployment, alcohol and other abuse, Principal A knew that such sudden confrontations will not disappear swiftly; if left unchecked they will quickly degenerate into the kind of 'incident' recorded earlier in this chapter. A key factor in this principal's handling of such incidents was that he communicated an essential person-to-person sense of equality, while also maintaining his principal's authority. Where there might be any evidence of low self-worth, he wanted to change that. The way to convert anger is not to suppress it, but to give it proper voice: 'individuals with a high self-esteem will appreciate and accept themselves in a realistic way – self-assertive individuals do not submit to domination by others, nor do they feel consciously superior to others' (Kalliopuska 1990: 123).

Leading by example

It is not easy to define those crucial conditions of 'willingness to work', which are so remarkably present in successful schools, and can be so disappointingly absent in others. Although there were differences of leadership style among the three principals, ranging from informal to relatively formal, there was in all three schools a strong emphasis on decorum, during school hours. The rich, colourful classrooms and comfortable social and working climate show that these were schools which encouraged application and absorption in learning tasks. Moreover, the willingness of these principals to lead by example was encapsulated in one small incident, where the principal of School C walked away from us in the playground of the school towards a boy who was yelling at another group of children. Within the space of a minute he communicated, first, his clear displeasure at the boy's shouting, then a willingness to listen to his explanation, followed by advice on how to put things right and an arrangement to follow up the incident at the end of the school morning. Similarly, the principal of School B explained that she was inadvertently late for our interview because she had been out with the local police officer, to collect a child who was missing from school, see his parent and bring him back to the school. Such common incidents as these which, if left unchecked, quickly become critical, bring home what it actually means, to be put daily on the line, in getting the arts of communication exactly right – through listening, talking, action and follow-up.

Getting it right with learners

For historical and social reasons, Aboriginal communities have suffered profound harm, over two hundred years, to their cultures and to their self-esteem. The harm is evident in the problems that Aboriginal students encountered during their progress (or, it must be admitted, regression) through the westernized education system. This is a system that Aboriginal communities acknowledge that they need, in order to compete on fair terms with all other groups in the nation. It would, however, be foolish to forget the extraordinary high cultural levels that Aboriginal communities have already achieved. The great Obiri Rock of Northern Australia, which was discovered by non-Aboriginal researchers only in the 1960s,

> is a cathedral of the Gagadju and Kunwinijku peoples whose galleries of paintings are here. The significance of these paintings has been compared with the deciphering of the Rosetta Stone with which the secrets of ancient Egypt are locked. The Obiri paintings predate the Pharaohs by twenty thousand years. They are more sophisticated than the cave drawings at Lascaux in France, by which the European tribes have measured their civilization.
>
> (Pilger 1989: 24)

This rock is now included belatedly in the World Heritage list; the Obiri's galleries of paintings are said to be 'perhaps the oldest and most significant expression of human creativity . . . the longest record of any group of people' (Souter and Stearman 1988: 5). Yet, as is revealed in many Australian reports on levels of achievement in language, the performance of Aboriginal and Torres Strait Islander students is significantly lower than that of the rest of the population.

Studies of school and teacher attitudes to Aboriginal students have revealed evidence of teachers who are 'unsupportive and may actively obstruct' the efforts of students (Partington *et al*. 1997). Day (1992) reported that, for most Aboriginal students, teacher relations were negative; teachers had low expectations of them, and lacked training in Aboriginal studies. In their detailed study of teacher attitudes to and interactions with school students in an urban setting, Dent and Hatton (1996: 50) noted 'strong derogatory deficit views' of both Aboriginal and Anglo-Australian working class children. Having labelled their backgrounds as 'bad', the teachers 'believe that students from bad backgrounds, not only suffer from limited money for education, poor nutrition and so on, but that they also have a poorer standard of language and a poorer capacity for academic success'. Dent and Hatton (1996: 59) conclude that teachers fail with these groups through the combined effects of the teachers' 'homogeneous backgrounds and inadequate initial preparation for social and cultural diversity that they encounter in schools'. A similar picture emerges in the UK, where over half of school exclusions are of children from black or ethnic minority groups, even though they make up less than a third of the school population. For Afro-Caribbean children, this figure stretches to nearly four times their actual number in the population, and the number of boys excluded reaches seven to eight times (Lawrence and Hayden 1997: 69).

Not surprisingly, teachers who are genuinely working to improve the quality of education for Aboriginal students wish to dispute such findings, at least from their own perspectives. The principal of School C, for example, claimed that such criticism 'is soul destroying for schools' personnel who are working hard to improve the quality of educational attainment of Aboriginal students . . . the fundamentals of good schools are the same in schools that teach Aboriginal students as for any other school'. That is true; yet it is also true that social inclusivity through recognition of distinct linguistic and cultural identities of different communities in Australia must also be an important component in educational provision (Barratt-Pugh *et al*. 1996).

So, what is needed to achieve an inclusive approach here? A good, concluding insight into this was provided by Caroline, a newly appointed teacher at School A. She declared that she enjoyed working in the school a great deal; in particular, she thought that all staff had the 'right attitude' to students and to parents. She put great stress on the importance of this attitude of essential equality, as a fundamentally different professional approach from those that she had encountered within the city. She stressed that students on initial teacher education (ITE) courses needed, above all, to know about the actual way that people (especially in Aboriginal communities) lived in a remote area, and that ITE tutors should place rather less emphasis on 'more exotic aspects of language and culture'. She described how she discovered only gradually, for example, that many of her students could sometimes be traumatized by what was known locally as a 'drama' (for example, a fight or drunken and disorderly conduct in the community). She advised that recent ex-students should be invited back on ITE courses, to explain just how things were in the field and that this might help to close the gap between 'telling' students and actually 'showing' students what is happening there.

Returning to her important theme about the handling of parents and communities, she thought that people could lose respect for teachers if they treated parents as though 'they have got no sense'. The teachers in School A, in her view, tended to ask 'How can I fix it?', rather than being judgemental. She disclosed that she had nearly decided to withdraw from her university teaching course, following adverse experiences during practice in 'normal' schools, where she had found very few examples of the kind of support and respect for students and parents that, in her view, constitute a truly professional approach in teaching.

The voice of this young teacher is, perhaps, the best available testimony to the fact that her highly respected principal was indeed leading by example. Serious problems persist, in school retention rates and in motivation and achievement for Aboriginal students; only one-third of Aboriginal and Torres Strait Islander students continue to Year 12, in contrast to over three-quarters of non-Aboriginal students (Partington *et al.* 1997). Inadequate schooling continues the cycle of poverty and failure for this community. Each of these three schools confronts these problems daily, and each is gradually succeeding in its clear determination to ensure that schools can make a genuine difference on behalf of their students, through succeeding in their genuine aims to improve the quality of communication with their clients – the students, their parents, and their community.

4

THE DESKILLERS AND THE
EMPOWERERS

We once heard of a senior member of a university department who had the reputation of always giving lower grades for students' work than anyone else. In his view, standards were always falling (he had been saying that for 20 years or more) and the department was admitting students who were intellectually inferior. His record of losing research students was regrettably high. In his view, that was never anything to do with his attitude; it was always that the students allocated to him were not capable of carrying out post-graduate research. Numerous efforts to point out that occasionally he might be at fault were invariably received with disbelief.

It was a cause for celebration when he went to China on a visit and for a brief period, peace reigned. Over coffee, one colleague said, 'You can just imagine him, can't you? There he is looking up at the Great Wall of China, and he's saying "Yes. Well. A good wall, but a great wall? Oh dear me no. Needs more work".' His attitude, and that of all others who look for weakness before strength in others can have a profound effect not only on individuals' self-esteem and academic performance, but, far more seriously, on their personal and career development. If students or employees are consistently told that they are inferior, there is a strong possibility that they will come to believe it. Justified or not, such a belief can follow them throughout life, as was made clear from the reported experiences of a number of speakers and delegates at a conference on leadership qualities.

The keynote address, given by Carol H, the headteacher of a primary school, left no doubt about what she considered to be the duties of a leader at any level. She drew, with some passion, on her own experience of working with bad and good leaders to illustrate her position.

> I trained to teach in my thirties and when I got a teaching post in a primary school locally, I was delighted. When I turned up for work on my first day as a teacher, I was excited and was really looking forward to it. It took one term of that head-teacher's regime to convince me I was useless. It took me one year to become totally deskilled. When she retired, a new head came and everything changed. If she hadn't retired when she did, I should have been out of teaching for ever. I had reached the stage where I couldn't have stood another week, let alone years of a life like that. I look back and think I shall never forgive that woman. Never.

Carol subsequently proved to be an outstanding teacher and head. Her school received top rating from an inspection team, and she was in demand locally and nationally as a speaker on improving the quality of teaching and the promotion of learning. So, what went wrong in her first teaching post? She knew precisely what went wrong, though at the time, she was convinced (or brainwashed to believe) that her apparent failure was entirely her fault. She recalled the atmosphere in the school with some anger:

> Nobody ever came into my classroom, and I never saw any of the other teachers teach. The children were a bit lively, but there was nothing wrong with them really. I made some mistakes in my early days by trying to treat them like lovely little angels who would listen to my every word with the keenest interest. I needed a bit of guidance and I got none. There was one child who was sometimes disruptive and when she was in that frame of mind, some of the others joined in. On one occasion, I mentioned this to one of the other teachers and asked if she had any suggestions. She didn't, but at the end of the school day, the headteacher sent a message that she wanted to see me, and she said that if I couldn't keep order, perhaps I should look for

another job. I was devastated. I never asked anyone else for advice, and never received any. I think what shocked me was that a colleague would go straight to the head and tell her I had discipline problems.

She still remembered her feeling of complete isolation. There was neither social contact nor professional support. She was quickly told if anything was wrong, but never that something had been done well. The headteacher stayed in her room all day, sent 'masses of memos ordering this or that', and never lost an opportunity to sneer at the inadequacies of a university which would 'hand out first-class degrees to people who couldn't teach'. She demanded total loyalty to her, as head of the school, but never behaved in a way which earned loyalty.

Life was transformed when the new head arrived. Carol vividly remembered the first day of the new regime:

The first thing the new head did was to walk into my room, and she said 'I hear you're a terrific teacher. My neighbours' children have been in your class and they used to sing your praises all the time. Do you mind if I join you tomorrow? Just tell me what you want me to do and I'll do it alongside the classroom assistant.' At the time, I was terrified, but that was the beginning of my rehabilitation. She taught herself, and that gave us some free time to prepare. She was in and out of classes all the time and she really did know how things were going. She encouraged all of us to improve our qualifications, to attend courses and conferences, to work together, and she worked with us. Teams were formed to develop various new areas of the curriculum, though not without opposition. Gradually, they began to work and we began to talk to each other.

There were a couple of teachers in that school who did the minimum amount of work and could always find a reason for not attending meetings or helping with events. They were quickly sorted out – and I admired that. I learnt a lot from both those heads. The first experience was devastating; the second was empowering. I think the most amazing thing was that after a while, I suddenly realized I was enjoying my work.

Within five years of the new regime, Carol was a deputy head. In another two years, she was a head. As might be expected, she had strong views about the role of headteachers:

No member of my staff will ever be made to feel as inadequate as I did, but equally, no teacher will get away with shoddy work. No newly qualified teacher will be left without support and any teacher who is willing to work and who has the potential for a senior post will have my full support, even though it might mean losing one of the best teachers in the school. I learnt my lesson the hard way, but I shall never forget it.

In Carol's view, it was clearly the responsibility of heads, heads of department and principals to *provide* the opportunities for professional, career and personal development – and to encourage staff to move on, when they were ready. She agreed with West-Burnham (1992: 112) that 'empowering is the fundamental component of quality leadership: in essence it involves releasing the potential of individuals – allowing them to flourish and grow, to release their capacity for infinite improvement'.

Carol summarized her view of good leadership principles, based on her own early experience, as

- doing everything possible to create a school culture which promotes a collegial community
- ensuring that no newly qualified teacher is left without support and monitoring
- fostering an environment of openness so that anyone in difficulties feels able to ask for help
- trying always to be open to new views and ideas, difficult though that might be
- walking around, getting to know what is happening, and anticipating problems before they arise
- confronting difficult situations and working towards resolution
- giving praise where praise is due
- deciding (with staff) on priorities, establishing a tried and tested system of needs analysis, planning and delivering a sound staff development programme
- encouraging team working and learning from each other
- sharing information so that staff are aware of what is happening in the outside educational world
- trying always to empower rather than deskill.

In conclusion, she said 'trying' was the key word in her case. She felt she could honestly claim success in more than half of the eleven principles, but would probably be working to achieve the rest for the whole of her life as a headteacher.

The empowerment challenge

In the question and answer session that followed, one conference delegate, a senior and respected college lecturer, challenged a number of Carol's statements about the role of leaders in empowering others:

> In my view, you're wrong about a number of things. For a start, you can't empower people who don't want to be empowered. I agree that professional development is essential so that we can all do our jobs well, but the needs of the college come first. As far as personal development is concerned, that's our business. If we want to take a higher degree, that's up to us. If we want promotion, we have to work at it. It's the head of department's or principal's job to make sure we attract and keep the best teachers. If we've got the best people, then the college and the students will be successful. If not, it will fail, no matter what systems are in place.

Perhaps surprisingly, he was supported by almost half the audience. Whitaker (1997: 22) appears to agree with them: it is the responsibility of individuals 'to take increasing responsibility for the satisfying of their personal and professional needs.' He continues: 'empowerment places emphasis on the individual for creating his or her own conditions for growth, for defining challenges and for setting goals and targets'.

In Carol's experience, it would have been impossible to have created her own conditions for growth under the regime of her first headteacher. Her concern was survival in a hostile environment, and growth was impossible in the culture of that school. However, the challenger was not about to give up. He complained that his head of department was 'on the empowerment gravy train': Warming to his subject, he said,

> I don't want to be 'empowered', at least, not in your terms of being 'developed' so I can rise in the educational hierarchy. I want to stay in my present job. I like it and do it well and I want to keep doing it. In my college, we are always having to bail out teachers who are taking higher degrees and who are given time off to study. It causes immense resentment.

As an example of what he saw as the sins of empowerment, he declared:

Whenever we have anybody really good on the staff, the head of department's got them in a corner and she's saying 'Why don't you leave? There's a good job going at the college up the road. There'll never be any promotion here for years, if at all'. Can you believe it? She does it all the time. That's not empowerment. It's getting rid of our greatest assets. I call it depriving our students of really good teachers and sending them to one of our competitors.

He was supported by a number of other delegates, one of whom asked:

What about empowerment of those who know they are in the right job as teachers, who have a real commitment to their students, but who need just as much opportunity for further development as anybody who is really setting out to be a head or principal? What about less emphasis on those at the top of the hierarchy, and more on developing the leadership qualities of classroom teachers who require leadership skills every day of their lives? What about working towards performance-related pay for teachers?

Carol strongly denied that her view of empowerment was directed towards encouraging good teachers to leave, regardless of their career preferences, but she held to her view that if individuals were hoping to achieve a senior position at some stage, she regarded it as part of her job to encourage and support them; to provide an environment which allowed considered risks to take place; to encourage the learning of teachers as well as pupils. 'And', she continued, 'that applies to teachers who wish to remain teachers quite as much as to individuals who hope to become heads of schools or principals of colleges'.

Empowering (and paying) teachers

In the working groups which followed Carol's presentation, the discussion centred on the position of career teachers – people who wished to remain teachers, but whose salaries had an upper limit with few opportunities to go beyond the maximum. The UK government proposals to create an advanced teacher grade might well help in the drive to keep expert teachers in the classroom, though, as everyone agreed, establishing fair and sustainable criteria and conditions will inevitably be difficult.

There were similar reservations about the principle of performance-related pay structures, though most of those present could point to certain individuals in their school or college who were known not to pull their weight and 'should either be made to toe the line or get out'. Harry Tomlinson, former principal of a college and a strong advocate of performance-related pay, certainly appreciates the problems of devising a fair and sustainable system; yet he still feels strongly that efforts should be made to implement it. He writes:

> There is, in industry as in teaching, the real problem of balancing intrinsic and extrinsic rewards for work, but that does not mean that extrinsic rewards can be ignored. A reward system should reinforce good performance, even if this is not necessarily the ideal place to start. All payment systems have flaws and may produce unintended or undesired behaviour. The present pay system for teachers rewards those who leave the classroom and become administrators, and thus works actively against encouraging excellence in classroom performance.... An incentive should link defined levels of performance to defined levels of pay.
>
> (Tomlinson 1992: 2)

So, in Tomlinson's view, the designation of 'expert teacher' or the introduction of a performance-related pay structure would reward the best teachers and provide a career structure for them which did not involve a move into management and administration. However, as he commented at an Open University staff development meeting, 'no one seems to agree with me about performance-related pay, so it may never happen'. Yet if it did, as one member of the group said,

> it would give 'empowerment' a special and down-to-earth meaning – helping teachers to become experts at their job rather than pushing them towards administration. Something recognized as more than the normal run of 'ordinary' career teacher, not only from the point of view of prestige, but also of cash. To be 'just a teacher' for the whole of working life seems to be regarded by some people as a failure. Money matters.

No one disagreed with that. Money does matter, but empowerment can take many different forms, as was illustrated by several members of the group who had had deskilling or empowering experiences when they were working towards MA, MEd or PhD degrees.

Supervisors and student researchers

An investigation into the progress of part-time students who were taking or had succeeded in obtaining postgraduate research degrees provided many similar examples (Bell 1996). The Bell study identified six major areas of influence which supported or impeded students' achievements:

- administration, information, support and facilities for postgraduate students
- students' previous experience of research
- problems relating to the quality of writing
- the particular circumstances of part-time mature research students (such as the demands of work and home)
- the wide variation in the approach of supervisors
- isolation.

Of these, perhaps unsurprisingly, the quality of supervision was considered to be of the greatest importance. The research student–supervisor relationship is very different from that of headteacher–teacher, but interviews with students and supervisors revealed many similar images of deskilling and empowering encounters. Several interviewees had had good and bad experiences similar to those described by Carol.

The vast majority of students interviewed had enjoyed very positive relationships with supervisors. Their comments were on the lines of 'very helpful'; 'taught me what research was all about'; 'could not have done this without her'; 'she made me believe I could do it, saw me through the bad times, read all my drafts carefully, was straight about what I had written and what more needed to be done'. One student, who had become good friends with her supervisor, wrote 'I resented her pushing and shoving at times when I was overwhelmed with work, but she was determined I'd finish – and when I did, she seemed as pleased as I was.'

In Carol's terms, these would be the empowerers. However, the deskillers were also at work. Where things went wrong, they went badly wrong, and students' comments were on the lines of 'could never get hold of him'; 'never returned my calls'; 'made me feel inadequate'; 'showed no signs of having read any of my drafts'; 'didn't seem to feel he had any responsibility for supervising my work or advising about my approach' and 'went on study leave, never told me, and no one was allocated to "take me over" at a crucial time in my research when I really needed help'.

One successful PhD student wrote with feeling about her experience of what she saw as one really humiliating and one supportive, helpful supervisor. Referring to her first supervisor, she wrote:

That man made me feel stupid. A tutorial with him (a rarity) convinced me that I wasn't up to it. I cannot recall one occasion when he felt anything I had done was worth anything. He very nearly destroyed me. I asked for a change of supervisor after one dreadful year. My request was not well received (the department was obviously not interested in troublemakers), but in the end I was allocated to someone in another department. After that, things improved. The new supervisor made me feel good, though she could be pretty critical at times. I left her tutorials on a high, determined to get on with the work. I suppose you could say she empowered me. I got my PhD last year and now have a temporary university lectureship which I hope will become permanent. Believe me, that first experience will remain with me for life – and should actually make me a very good supervisor. I have experienced the very best and the very worst.

The supervisor concerned objected strongly to being classified as 'an empowerer'. She said, in some irritation,

Why do you use words like empowerment? It's just a fudge and unhelpful. If I take on responsibility for supervising a student, it is not an optional extra. It's serious work. I spend time on it. There's a code of conduct for supervisors in this university, which I have actually read, but I just do the job as I see it. Supervision is a joint activity. I can't make students do anything, nor can I write their thesis, but I do my best to help them along and to prevent them from wasting time going down blind alleys. We jointly set targets and I expect students to reach them in all but the most extreme circumstances. Some students object to that. Supervision takes time, doesn't count for much in the university and not all my colleagues feel supervision is at the top of their list of priorities. That's the way it goes.

She is not the only person to object to the term 'empowerment'. Many of the conference members objected equally strongly and felt the use of 'that word' had led to time wasting arguments about meaning and interpretation and took up valuable time from the key issues of leadership qualities, which were the focus of the conference.

So what is empowerment?

Is it any more than a fancy name for doing a good job as a leader, manager or supervisor, or is an empowerer just an all-round good egg who is always willing to help anyone who needs just a bit of support? A woolly concept to make something ordinary sound 'academic' and 'theoretical', or just plain common sense? Is it 'lifting a person's vision to higher sights, the raising of a person's performance to a higher standard, the building of personality beyond its normal limitations' (Drucker 1977: 370–1)? And does it matter what it means anyway, as long as the people who use it know what they mean and how they interpret 'empowerment' in the context of their work?

Definitions abound. Hopson and Scally (1981: 57), writing about life skills, considered self-empowerment was 'a process by which one increasingly takes greater charge of oneself and one's life', but Carol had made clear that if the culture of an organization is entirely negative, if there is no shared understanding of where the organization is heading, then no growth can take place. Hopson and Scally agree, but they continue by asserting that 'behaviour will be self-empowered only if it embodies certain values' (1981: 60).

Coulson-Thomas (1997: 175) supports this view and warns, 'unless vision, values, goals and objectives are communicated and shared, their impact if any is likely to be limited to those who formulated them'. He continues:

> Empowerment is about building local authority, accountability and ownership and creating circumstances in which inhibitors and constraints are removed, thus allowing the former to be responsibly exercised. It is not about giving a general licence to people to do what they please. It should not result in an abdication of responsibility, and however it is accomplished, some form of organisational structure is likely to remain.
>
> (Coulson-Thomas 1997: 256–7)

Coulson-Thomas was writing about management practice in Xerox, where the view was that people must be 'empowered, trained and work in an environment that reflects the value they represent for Xerox; and for those on the receiving end, "empowerment" is being energized, committed and enabled to autonomously achieve continuous quality improvement in work processes and outputs' (p. 257).

So, in the view of the Xerox managers, empowerment is a necessary attribute for a successful industry; in the commercial and industrial context it appears to relate entirely to the need to get the best out of people *in the interests of the organization.*

Murgatroyd and Morgan (1992), writing about total quality management and the school, present a view of empowerment which is closely related to business practice:

> Basic empowerment begins when the vision and goals have already been set by the school leaders. What a team or an individual is empowered to do is to turn the vision and strategy into reality through achieving those challenging goals set for them by the leadership of the school. Individuals are being empowered in terms of how they can achieve the goals set, not in terms of what the goals might be.
>
> (Murgatroyd and Morgan 1992: 21)

This would appear to be some way from the notion of 'lifting a person's vision to higher sights' and 'the building of a personality beyond its normal limitations' (Drucker 1977: 371) and 'releasing the potential of individuals – allowing them to flourish and grow' (West-Burnham 1992: 112).

Bottery (1995), referring to the Murgatroyd and Morgan Total Quality Management (TQM) approach, argues persuasively that

> One might argue that it is precisely in this area that schools and colleges differ from business, for if one of their key features is the need for them to develop the citizens of the future, then part of this development must be in precisely the development of empowerment – where empowerment means the nurturing and encouragement of ideas and visions which comes from within, not simply the implementation of others' visions.
>
> (Bottery 1995: 41)

But what if the nurturing of individual, personal vision and values are in direct collision with those of managers and colleagues? What if seriously self-focused individuals decide that other people can go to the devil as far as they are concerned, and that the values and goals of the organization have no place in their career plans? Given a sufficiently strong will and an unusually thick skin, they can make life very difficult for everyone. And let's not be too starry eyed about this; such individuals, though rare, do exist.

We are reminded of the joke about a shipwrecked sailor who, walking to safety up the beach of his desert island, met the island's Man Friday. He asked,

'Is there a government here?'
'Yes,' said Man Friday.
'I'm agin it,' said the sailor.

Those who are 'agin' everything, on principle, generally have their own personal agenda, which concentrates on their own values and their own particular brand of 'self-empowerment'. They will generally give leaders and colleagues considerable grief and will test leadership qualities to the limit. But Hopson and Scally (1981: 60) consider that such behaviour cannot be called 'self-empowerment'. They refute the concern of some doubters that 'self-empowered people are likely simply to be more selfish and more skilled in their abilities to manipulate others' because, they assert, 'by our definition this could not be so as a vital element in the concept of self-empowerment is the desire and ability to enable others to achieve more power over their own lives'.

But is this just playing with words? It would seem that 'empowerment' can mean whatever anyone wants it to mean:

- the commitment of one individual (such as a research degree supervisor) to another (the student)
- the development of workers in order to ensure the success of the organization
- the determination of an education leader to develop a culture in which professional, career and personal growth can take place.

It is probably immaterial what words are used as long as leaders understand the responsibilities they have towards their colleagues, the damage they can do by sometimes unintended deskilling practices, and the difference they can make to the lives of people who are given the opportunity to learn, develop, and to participate. Drucker (1977) makes it clear where he stands on the responsibilities of leaders and managers:

A manager who starts out by assuming that people are weak, irresponsible and lazy will get weakness, irresponsibility and laziness. A manager who assumes strength, responsibility and desire to contribute may experience a few disappointments. But the first task of managers is to make effective the strengths

of people. And this they can do only if they start out with the
assumption that people . . . want to achieve.

(Drucker 1977: 348)

This sounds so obvious that it might be taken for granted that
all managers would without question work towards this desirable
state. However, managers to whom we have spoken are clear that
though they agree, in principle, it is not always easy to achieve and
maintain such an ideal environment in practice. Moreover, several
defended their corner by saying that if they experience too many
disappointments, then goodwill and belief in people can disappear.

Carol's last word

Carol had begun the conference with the denouncement of her first
headteacher and her gratitude to her second. Drawing the conference to a close, she again referred to these two experiences which
had had such an influence on her professional life, and reminded
her conference colleagues that the deskillers were still around – in
education and in industry and commerce. The problem was, she felt,
that they did not always recognize themselves as deskillers. She
presented Kanter's (1983) ten rules for stifling initiative and block-
ing change in business organizations, most of which, she considered,
applied perfectly well to education – and to her own experience.

1 Regard any new idea from below with suspicion – because it's
   new and because it's from below.
2 Insist that people who need your approval to act first go through
   several other levels of management to get their signatures.
3 Ask departments or individuals to challenge and criticize each
   other's proposals. (That saves you the job of deciding; you just
   pick the survivor.)
4 Express your criticisms freely and withhold your praise. (That
   keeps people on their toes.) . . .
5 Treat identification of problems as signs of failure, to discour-
   age people from letting you know when something in their area
   isn't working.
6 Control everything carefully. Make sure people count anything
   that can be counted, frequently.
7 Make decisions to reorganize or change policies in secret, and
   spring them on people unexpectedly. (That also keeps people
   on their toes.)

8 Make sure that requests for information are fully justified and make sure it is not given out . . . freely. (You don't want data to fall into the wrong hands.)

9 Assign to lower-level managers, in the name of delegation and participation, responsibility for figuring out how to cut back, lay off, move people around, or otherwise implement threatening decisions you have made. And get them to do it quickly.

10 And, above all, never forget that you, the higher-ups, already know everything important about this business.

(Kanter 1983: 101)

Carol concluded by saying:

> I have been told by a number of people during the course of this conference that no headteacher could have behaved in such a crass way as I depicted in my first experience – but I did not exaggerate. Some of you may feel that these ten rules for stifling initiative are a caricature of dreadful practice, and could never happen, but just give some thought to your own experience, and what made any of your teachers or managers particularly good (or bad). Then you just might be able to relate your own experience to one or other of these 'rules', as I have done.
>
> I have also been told that the difference between deskillers and empowerers lies in the personality of the individuals concerned – the way they approach their jobs and the regard they have for their colleagues and their students. 'Get the right people in the top jobs', I have been told, 'and everything will be all right'. I agree, but that has proved to be harder to achieve than might be supposed. And no matter who is up there at the top, I hope it does not mean that they have nothing further to learn from their successes and their failures – nor from the successes and failures of others.

It would certainly be a frightening prospect for the future if we ever felt there was nothing left for us to learn.

Postscript

It is very easy to be critical about what are considered by some to be poor management or leadership principles and practices, but the view is sometimes different from the other side of the fence.

During the course of the conference, a good many different views were expressed, some of which provided strong challenges to the beliefs expressed by speakers. One speaker's claim that his head of department was 'on the empowerment gravy train', and encouraged some of their best teachers to leave, was not lighthearted. He meant it. In his view, she gave her loyalty to some of the ambitious and high flying teachers, not to the students. That, to him, was disgraceful. Others did not agree. They felt she was doing a good job by encouraging able staff who hoped for promotion, to gain more experience by moving on. That difference of view was never resolved, nor is it ever likely to be resolved.

The question of loyalty was also raised by Carol in her keynote address. In her first school, it was the head who demanded loyalty from all her staff, though she appeared to have done nothing to deserve it. There will always be problems over the meaning of loyalty in different contexts, and to whom loyalty should be given, particularly in times of conflict. Should it be 'loyalty to students and parents, teachers, superiors, to a common curriculum, to personal pedagogical values?' (Møller 1996: 99). One speaker had no doubt that loyalty should be to students, but his head of department challenged the view that loyalty was one-dimensional. She categorically denied that in supporting colleagues who wished to rise up the management ladder, she was adversely affecting students' learning.

Carol's first head had looked to her informers to tell her tales so that she could then pull rank by humiliating the offender. The second head created an environment which was sufficiently open for problems to be aired and trust to be established and as a result, loyalty was given, not only to the school, but also to her. It takes time and sensitivity to establish the sort of environment which admits loyalty.

5

LEARNING TO SHED OLD SKINS: COLLABORATING FOR CHANGE

This chapter considers two principles in the management of educational change. The first concerns the importance of optimism in believing that nearly all people can respond to demands for change, and can transform themselves, when they understand why change must happen. The second concerns what it means to be a 'good academic' or, more abstractedly, what constitutes continuity of excellence for the emerging new professional in universities.

The chapter provides an account of the review of a faculty of education in an Australian university which is on the move, from its earlier traditional role as a provider of initial teacher education programmes, to its present, more complex roles. These include provision of a wide range of advanced educational studies, post-school training and development, and flexible multimedia education, as well as new forms of initial teacher education programmes. There is also a vigorous emergence of research activity and output, which has made a considerable impact on the changing identity of the faculty.

Prior to the faculty review, some important pressures for reform were considered, which universities worldwide are now having to face; this required the faculty to confront longstanding questions about the 'idea' of a university.

Changing ideas of a university

In the competitive 1990s, older, larger, successful universities have to an extent been able to exploit the market value of their long established reputations, while younger, aspiring universities have made a virtue of their newness and have asserted their vitality and flexibility in meeting demands for change. Universities have slowly come to accept that they must adopt business disciplines in order to succeed, and that they must be committed to satisfying the needs of their clients in the community. However, communities – including businesses themselves – also look to universities to *be* universities. Not unreasonably, they expect universities, like all educational institutions, to be ethically and effectively managed, and to continue to provide high quality, cost-effective research and teaching, in order to meet changing community needs. As Pring (1997) has argued, an important aspect of their commitment to communities is their special responsibility in developing professional and vocational as well as academic excellence. They have a distinctive role in serving the cause of social justice, as well as encouraging educational diversity. Allied to all these, and emerging from them, is the belief that success in developing new modes of teaching and learning should enable universities to make a crucial impact on building quality lifelong learning for all, and a renewed share of professional purpose for universities (Nixon *et al.* 1997). If these roles are to be fulfilled, then universities of the future will need not only to serve the changing requirements of the community, but also to support their staff in developing new professional/academic roles. It follows, therefore, that leaders must retain their concern for issues of human value, in their desire to achieve high quality research and teaching. It will be through people that successful reform will happen and the task of leaders will necessarily be to create 'a resilient human resource amidst tough worldwide competition' (Ow Yong Kean Guan 1995: 48). The question is to what extent university staff are ready to embark on this path to self-responsibility.

To be a successful university in this period, 'you must be successfully reformed, and seen to be reformed (Marginson 1996: 118). Yet, despite a general acceptance of such rhetoric among university academics, there persists a widespread view that they prefer safe, if long-worn, comforts of the past, to the exciting, if dangerous, present. For example, writing on higher education's new status as a mature industry, Levine (1997: A48) reviewed changes in US government and community attitudes to higher education, which

– whether academics like it or not – have shifted from concerns with educational processes, to a concern with outcomes. Levine argued that higher education is adjusting too slowly to its new status as a mature industry, which cannot expect to enjoy continuous growth in the future. The same questions that the US government is putting to its universities and colleges may be found throughout the world. Levine's checklist of questions on productivity and efficiency includes

• How much should the faculty teach?
• How much should it cost to educate a student?
• Can campuses be replaced by new technologies?

He accuses academics in higher education of failing to face crucial issues of matching costs to outcomes. If they continue to evade this, it will 'prompt businesses which have criticized higher education for its high cost and low productivity, to challenge colleges by offering more of their own programs and degrees. One way or another, we are now ripe for a takeover by public or private forces'. If universities do not wish to be regarded by governments or by communities as 'arrogant' or 'self-serving', then they must match costs to outcomes, and not simply keep on putting off the day of reckoning through trying to raise yet more money by increased student charges or other escape routes. In short, the quest for high quality higher education must be the same as the quest for cost-effectiveness in higher education.

The move to globalization and multimedia expertise

Levine's criticisms will be familiar to university and college leaders. The pressures for change that he identifies explain why universities now aim towards globalization and multimedia expertise. These are their routes to competitiveness and cost-effectiveness, and faculty staff must make their academic plans accordingly. Tinkler *et al.* (1996: xvi) noted that university teachers 'will need to become more technologically literate . . . more willing to debate issues exposed by new communication systems, and less inclined to be content with established educational practices'.

Such points are now familiar in the research literature on new educational technologies throughout education. In higher education, the rapid development of new technologies has led to important policy developments as reviewed in the report by the Association of European Universities (AEU 1997) on *Universities and the Challenge of New Technologies*. Conclusions of the report include recommendations that

- Experimentation in flexible/distance learning programmes should be seen as part of the academic strategy of a university to *fulfil its mission*, not as an end in itself.
- Quality issues should cover teaching materials, delivery methods, students' work and, most important, the *learning process*.
- Universities should develop successful pilot projects into *full operational schemes*, and adapt experience gained at postgraduate levels to undergraduate studies.
- New technologies for teaching and learning will need appropriate *new structures*, to ensure a coherent framework.
- The roles (and professional development) of the university tutors must change (to be *interactive*); also the roles of students (to be more *independent*).
- Collaboration/partnership between universities and other organizations will reinforce concepts of the university as a *network organization*, or 'learning broker'.

All this involves important adjustments to university teachers' relations with students, in moving from expert status to guide status, and from didactic modes to dialogue and co-learning. These changes are not easy for those who are used to planning structures and processes that have been 'crafted for a slower pace of change. The cycle of academic change must be substantially shortened for the Information Age' (Dolence and Norris 1995: 85). That significant innovation is already happening is evidenced in Yetton *et al.* (1997: 73), although such innovation is often achieved in the face of what Yetton's team terms as 'resistance' to information technology (IT).

The new professionalism and stirring the pot for cultural change

It has become apparent, as Nixon *et al.* (1997: 5) point out, that 'the new management of education requires a new professionalism'. Cultural changes in universities through technology and globalization are accelerating, whether or not their staff may be ready for them. Moreover, the changes involve big business, as Australia has witnessed, where Australian vice-chancellors rejected Telstra, the government-owned telecommunications authority, and in 1997, chose the private sector competitor Optus to manage the Australian Academic Research Network (AARNet). Deals at this level involve sums estimated to be in excess of US$70 million, and will affect all higher education teaching and research in Australia. Many universities can already claim a high degree of expertise in new learning technologies among their staff and students: 'in two years, most of US science undergraduates at major universities have travelled the web learning curve. In the computer field, the UK is not much more than a year behind the US' (Venables 1997: iv–v). These dramatic changes have profound implications for everyone in higher education and particularly for leaders. The challenges for change which now face universities require, among other things, planning in two key directions:

- new kinds of *teaching/learning resources* (in particular, new education and multimedia technologies)
- new *staffing policies* (in particular, new modes of recruitment and of professional development).

The ways in which these dual directions for planning will stir the organizational pot may be seen in these terms, which link staffing policies (S) with new high quality teaching modes (T), new information/educational technologies (I), and research enhancement (R), as illustrated in Figure 5.1.

Any cultural shift requires careful planning of new staffing policies, including full opportunities for professional development of existing staff, and careful analysis of need in the recruitment of new staff. Then, the expectation is that through these two crucial, interlinked planning processes, departments will enable their staff to work towards enhancing both their teaching and their research. Through linking sound research with innovative teaching, they are likely to be in a position to achieve satisfaction among their students, among professions and communities, and even (we may hope) with governments. Laudable ambitions, but any fundamental cultural shift requires a series of deep breaths and a determination to succeed. It also requires a significant number of innovators who believe in the need for change and who are prepared to take on a leadership role in implementing change.

Eastcott (1996: 12) offers a quite optimistic picture of organizational adjustment to change, where a small number of innovators may expect to win over half the workforce quite quickly, and may eventually attract a substantial majority (though it is recognized that some may never adjust): see Figure 5.2.

Figure 5.1 STIRring the organizational pot

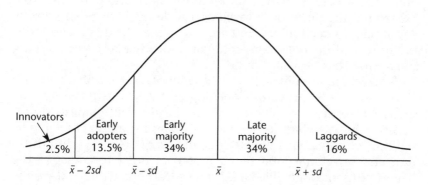

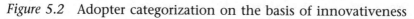

Figure 5.2 Adopter categorization on the basis of innovativeness

Change through new educational technologies

Discussion about change through new educational technologies is not new; the hard task is to transform discussion into action for change. Many educational leaders must have wondered, 'if only' they could make a fresh beginning, with no baggage from the past. The rare chance of a quite fresh beginning does occur, now and then, as was the case in the early 1970s, with the then newly established Open University in the UK. At that time, the Open University was regarded with some condescension, if not disapproval, by traditional universities. As Britain's first 'teaching only' university, how could it be a serious university institution, without a research base? However, university academics quickly discovered that the Open University was producing quality course materials which they adopted, sometimes surreptitiously, and on which their students thrived. This was not surprising, since the Open University's materials provided a dramatic improvement on the standard lectures and handouts that prevailed in those times. The process of being an Open University course team member is not a comfortable experience: all drafts are subject to vigorous criticism from colleagues and from external assessors. Furthermore, course units and modules have a shared, not individual ownership.

The Open University is now an internationally respected mega-university, with its own powerful research base, and with an enviable reputation in such key fields as educational technology, educational management and administration, and curriculum development in education, as well as a wide range of other science, social science, technology and arts disciplines. Its direct and indirect influence on both conventional and other distance learning universities has been profound.

Changes are usually achieved at some cost – to individuals and to organizations. Instead of opening as a new institution (as the Open University was able to do), an already well established university is likely to have experienced pain and strain in changing its outlook, culture, teaching patterns, modes of delivery, administration and secretariat (and much more), in order to adjust to the new conditions of flexible and distance learning, while at the same time conserving key areas of existing strength.

The role of the modern university

The forces that compel universities to move with all urgency towards cultural change are unlikely to make innovative academic leaders patient with the laggards. Universities acknowledge that it is they who must lead any transformation in higher education, and yet their essential academic task remains the same: they must produce the 'wise intellectuals who will lead us all to the future' (Stokes 1997).

Reflecting on the role that a modern university should play, Nicholson (1997) emphasized how vocational and academic expertise must be interwoven:

> The university's function is . . . essentially not just to collect, store and impart knowledge but to do so in a way which cultivates the intellect of the student and the researcher. It is important that a university is a source of training but it is essential that it is a source of ideas; ideas expressed because they are perceived and not because they are palatable. It is the cultivation of the intellect in a way which sharpens critical facilities, arouses an interest in further knowledge and creates the personal internal momentum for further intellectual activity that is truly the function of the University.
>
> (Nicholson 1997: 6)

We agree that universities must serve their communities well, through meeting vocational and professional needs. We acknowledge that they must inevitably listen to government and community pressures to be more accountable for providing high quality, but also cost-conscious research and teaching. We understand they must become more flexible, more globalized, more clever in using multimedia technologies. Yet, in swimming with a strong tide of change, it is important that universities must not lose their nerve, nor their distinctive identity. In this they rely, more crucially than is sometimes acknowledged, on an academic community which is empowered, through its own essential academic qualities, to make its distinctive contribution to what Nicholson described as 'the cultivation of the intellect'.

The essential debate about academic freedom is not a debate about tenure, or job protection. It is about the faculty member's freedom – to imagine, discover, report and consider new approaches to learning.

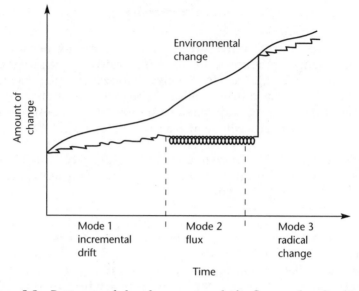

Figure 5.3   Patterns of development – drift, flux and radical change

Organizational culture

As was seen in Chapter 2, it is important to understand the cultural 'webs' (Johnson 1992) or 'imprints' (Irwin 1996) of an organization. Only through a context-specific understanding of a faculty and of its members can work begin to improve it. Johnson's useful paper sought to explain how dangerous gaps can develop between the culture of an organization and the environmental changes around it, which the organization may or may not have noticed. Johnson viewed patterns of strategic development in three modes, namely 'drift', 'flux' and 'radical change': see Figure 5.3.

In Mode 1, the environment is changing swiftly, but the organization is in a state of what Johnson terms 'incremental drift'. In Mode 2, the organization has become aware of the gap that is widening between its own cultural position and actual environmental changes. Understandably, this can cause confusion and loss of direction, or 'flux', as Johnson terms it. In Mode 3, change in the organization has to be made rapidly, causing possibly painful adjustments in order to close the gap that has emerged between culture and reality. Johnson (1992: 34) identified six factors that make up the cultural web or paradigm of an organization. Through cultural analysis and remedial action, he argued, it is possible to begin work on closing gaps between (often rapid) changes in the environment outside, and the 'incremental drift' of an organization that has failed to adapt to environmental change. For Johnson, culture needs to be understood in order to change it.

Irwin (1996), on the other hand, emphasized the importance of working *within* the pattern of cultural imprints, since it is unrealistic to try to change them through outside intervention: 'while culture is dynamic, many cultural imprints – passed on from generation to generation – seem to change very slowly if at all' (Irwin 1996: 2).

The art of effecting useful change, Irwin argued, is to decide where to intervene in the light of cultural patterns, rather than (following Johnson) taking straightforward action to reshape them. Invoking a study which was conducted for Telstra in Australia, Irwin identified what he claimed to be distinctive Australian cultural imprints. The Telstra study highlighted the following aspects of Australian culture which need to be understood by leaders of organizations:

- Quality (in, for example, teaching or research) is closely linked by Australians with an 'appreciation of their own identity and self-worth'. It is of 'fundamental' importance for leaders of Australian organizations to understand this.
- High quality work depends on attracting the willing participation of people, who feel that they work as 'volunteers' in their contribution to a team effort. Those who feel excluded from this tend to fall into three other categories:
  - the complainers or 'whingers'
  - the 'survivors/conscripts' who soldier on without achieving much
  - the 'prisoners' who feel trapped and deeply discontented in their work.

Whether these categories are specifically Australian is certainly debatable; Krell and Spich (1996: 66), for example, proposed several versions of 'lame ducks' in US organizations, including the 'unbeliever' (who cannot believe the realities to be faced); the 'good soldier' (who carries on regardless); the 'retired on the job' (who counts the days to a well earned pension); the 'passive hostile' (who is angry, and damages through omission); the 'active hostile' (who feels there is nothing to lose by any damage they can do); and the 'destroyer' (who takes every opportunity to 'get even' with the organization).

This somewhat grim picture of 'lame ducks' is, arguably, a distinctively American way of looking at people management; yet there are clear overlaps with the Telstra study. However, the Telstra categories are not presented as fixed attitudes, but as signs of a defensive emotional detachment in the excluded group, which may change swiftly when leaders work from a more clear understanding of the actual nature of the cultural imprints that the work group shares.

Irwin continues by suggesting additional Australian cultural characteristics:

- Australians value recognition and reward just as in other cultures, but they prefer praise to be 'sincere, perceived as well-deserved, and low-key'. Modes of praise which might be regarded as warm and generous throughout the Americas might be regarded as 'inappropriate and embarrassing' for Australians.
- Communication and feedback are certainly essential modes of building trust and understanding in a team. However, the Telstra study found that 'feedback' for Australians may be linked to 'bad news'. It is, therefore, important to avoid any sense of inquisition or blame, when providing feedback. Australians expect to receive a candid account of the facts of a problem, but this should not be overstated. Any exaggeration of dangers or difficulties to be faced may be met by the finely tuned 'bull-shit detectors' (to quote Irwin) that characterize Australian thinking.
- 'The most powerful way to motivate Australians to participate in change is to offer them a cause' – something which transcends being the 'biggest' or the 'best', and has desirable social, moral, national or community associations.

(Irwin 1996: 6–7)

Irwin's argument becomes useful when confronting the question: why is it important to understand the cultural imprints of faculty members, during times of educational change? The answers that Irwin suggests are worth keeping in mind, when returning to Johnson's more practical concerns of seeking to change organizational culture in order to meet environmental change. The 'why?' that Johnson asks is: why do some organizations find it more difficult than others to adjust to environmental change? He follows that with a 'what?': what cultural features of an organization need to be identified, in order to prepare to adjust that organization to the environment?

The cultural audit of the faculty of education

The changes in perception of 'what a university is, or should be, in modern times' influenced the approach to the faculty audit and overall review. Where appropriate, the initial faculty 'cultural audit' adopted headings proposed by Johnson (on the lines adopted in Chapter 2) as a means of identifying key areas requiring change. It should, by the way, be emphasized that, by the time of the audit, the faculty was already addressing many of the problems identified below; it had already moved from 'incremental drift' as defined by Johnson, to prepare for radical change.

Power structure

The faculty had a three-tier structure of dean's office, schools and departments, with strong formal traditions of line management (conversely, many questions were being raised about extending the sharing and ownership of decision making).

Organizational structure

There was an unwieldy committee structure (but a growing sense that 'something must be done'); no faculty strategic planning group in place, and no formal role for professors (though professorial objections to this had been heard); no formal structure for staff–student consultation (though students were regularly consulted on their experience of teaching); no formal structure for student support (though many tutors had excellent reputations in this field).

Control systems

There was a well defined budgeting system, but the faculty was weak on quality assurance systems in teaching and research (though research output was monitored through a 'reward' system, and there was scrutiny of funding applications for small-scale research, conferences and study leave).

Stories and myths

'It is wrong to try to introduce cost efficiency into teaching, because it is obvious that students need to spend as much time as possible with their tutors' (though some research-active staff were questioning whether three hour teaching sessions should be reduced to two hours); 'everyone – including the dean and professors – must take part in the practicum (teaching practice arrangements)', (countered by 'the practicum is a sacred but sick cow which must be reformed'); 'how things were in the old days, when there was no hassle about money' (in contrast to increasing pressure from some areas for a more fair allocation of funds across the faculty); 'our students are not as academically strong as in other faculties, and they need more spoon feeding' (but other tutors insisted that encouraging guided and independent learning was the best way of improving results); 'this faculty should base its reputation on its excellent teaching and not be too much concerned with research' (countered by an increasingly widely held view that 'it is only through research and development that innovative, high quality teaching can flourish').

Rituals and routines

'Staff tend to keep office hours, with extended mid-morning and mid-afternoon breaks' (but research-active staff had already become more flexible here); 'some new lecturers and managers who have tried to introduce new ideas need to learn more about the history of this place' (countered by the view that 'it is time now to move on from the past'); 'traditional format of lectures and fixed teacher led sessions' (but some faculty tutors were already teaching round-the-clock flexible programmes, both nationally and overseas, and using multimedia technology); 'traditional systems of assessment, dependent mainly on examinations' (yet some staff were engaged in highly imaginative and successful alternative modes of assessment); 'timetable dominated by practicum and assessment processes' (but these were being increasingly challenged); 'some reluctance to accept that regular feedback of student experience and criticism should influence teaching programmes' (yet good forms of consultation were already in place, on some courses).

Symbols

There were heavy, dark wood furnishings in the dean's office (but new purpose-built accommodation was now planned; meanwhile, minor improvements in this area will include, in particular, a 'welcome and waiting' area for faculty visitors); student and staff areas around the colleges quite strictly demarcated (but there was evidence of genuine respect, equality and friendship among some staff and students); décor in older parts was ageing (but walls of the colleges generously filled with many paintings of high quality by established and student painters); a shortage of signs or symbols which proclaim the presence of the faculty in a building.

Tackling the issues

Several issues emerging from this simple and partial audit were easy to address. For example, a Faculty Strategic Planning Group was soon in place, which included all heads of school and professors in the faculty; a staff–student committee was formed, which reported to the Heads of School Committee; and serious work began on improving quality assurance in teaching and in research.

Other issues could not be tackled so directly. Attention to accommodation and décor, for example, will have to wait until the faculty of education has its new purpose designed building (which was promised within three years). And, given the high average age of the faculty (over 52) long-lasting cultural attitudes to teaching and teaching quality were unlikely to shift quickly. One limited line of direct action, was, however, possible here. A favourable early retirement deal was negotiated with the local Taxation Office; this option was offered without pressure, and emphatically as a *choice* for individuals, to all staff aged over 55, which ten people accepted. Ironically, then, an early achievement in initiating change was to give the opportunity for a number of staff to leave the faculty. However, this provided a beginning, in making first plans for a new staffing strategy, in the light of new directions that are planned for teaching and research.

Why do you want to make life so uncomfortable for yourself and for us?

This and similar questions were put to members of the faculty in response to proposals to restructure the faculty by removing the middle tier of management and replacing it with flexible working teams. Other faculty members supported the restructure; unanimous formal approval by the faculty board was gained, following wide discussion of the proposals throughout the faculty. In a thoughtful chapter on a 'Gestalt for schools in the new millennium', Caldwell (1997: 269) urges educational leaders to develop the competency of 'thinking in time', in order not to be 'stranded in time'.

From the outset, the faculty could rely on excellent administrative and secretarial staff, and a number of highly accomplished academic leaders, who were willing to give new ideas a try. In practical terms, a small group was appointed to work on the restructuring of the faculty and, above all, to ensure that every individual member of the faculty, both academic and non-academic, was consulted. The group was selected to represent a range of views: a young researcher-teacher, a member of the 'old guard', an innovative head of department, a top fund-raising researcher, and so on. Arrangements were also made for critical issues in teaching, research and general faculty concerns to be investigated at various levels; this was by all staff, followed by a convening of thirty or so senior staff for a two-day 'retreat' in a hotel by the sea. One remarkable aspect of this was that many 'old guard' representatives who attended the staff retreat provided some of the most radical new proposals for change. There was no stubborn defending of entrenched positions. On the contrary, the sustained discussions – thoughtful, critical, challenging, often witty and lighthearted – removed barriers of age, status or gender among faculty members. It was agreed, unanimously, that the retreat should become an annual event and that it deserved a high priority, in terms of planning for its success. From this retreat, an agreed picture emerged of twelve key areas which needed urgent attention, in teaching, research and general faculty issues.

Teaching

In teaching, a 'force field' of four critical factors was identified as tending either to activate or to resist development in new fields. A plan of action accompanied each of the factors, as shown in Table 5.1.

It may be noted that the factors identified here are globally familiar. If they have not already done so, universities are now preparing urgently to develop flexibly delivered new teaching programmes (A1). Since they cannot take future government support of higher education for granted, they must now take full heed of cost, quality and student/client needs. Given an ever rising demand for highly educated and highly skilled teachers (A2), the pressure on them to be continuously engaged in professional development provides important opportunities for faculties of education. There will be a continued national demand for initial teacher education (A3). However, some countries – such as the UK – have sought during the 1990s to fund this ever more parsimoniously; some countries – such as Australia – remain undecided about predicting a shortage or oversupply of teachers in the near future. In the quest for teaching quality (A4), there is now a desperate search throughout higher education to establish effective quality assurance and control systems in all teaching programmes, which do not actually take longer to operate than the teaching programmes themselves. In order to highlight its concern to improve teaching quality, the faculty decided also to award twelve annual Excellence in Teaching awards to faculty members. The awards would be decided on criteria of teaching innovation and student experience of the teaching programme, and would carry a significant financial reward, to be spent on behalf of teaching improvement, in ways to be decided by recipients.

While the pressures to achieve high quality teaching are universal, the pressures that the faculty identified as resisting change may be specific to itself and the action to be taken may suit its particular conditions. In any case, it was acknowledged that teaching

Table 5.1 Teaching: critical factors and action plan

Force field of critical factors		Action plan
Activating development	*Resisting development*	
A1 Flexible programmes Demand for new modes of teaching/learning in education (in order to remove difficulties of distance; use new multimedia technologies).	Varying degrees of staff readiness for new modes; variable markets	Promote innovative research related modes of teaching. Strengthen national/ international partnerships (South-east Asia, Indian Ocean) – e.g. new MBA in Education Administration; advanced courses in TESOL/TENSE; Train-the-Trainers; Early Childhood.
A2 *Upgrading the teaching profession* A first degree no longer enough for essential success. Demand for higher degrees (MEd; PhD) in current studies programmes.	Research climate in the faculty needs to be developed, to strengthen advanced studies areas. Teaching profession needs to be made aware of career-long advanced studies opportunities.	Publicity/recruitment drive; staff development programmes (through a new Office for Teaching Quality); review/reduce fees for fee paying students; develop cost-effective courses (throughout all teaching programmes).

A3 *National/regional needs for initial teacher education*		
Demand for undergraduate programmes to increase (following growth of 17–19 age group), especially for early years/special needs.	Uncertainty about government policy on student recruitment; uncertain predictions for teacher recruitment – steady demand? Shortages to emerge after 2000?	Publicity/recruitment drive; develop early childhood/primary/secondary programmes. Streamline the practicum.
A4 *Quest for quality*		
Growing national/international demand for high quality undergraduate and postgraduate programmes.	Traditional teacher training culture may resist new quality standards.	Restructure responsibility for teaching quality within main programmes – primary; secondary; advanced. Ensure continuous quality review of courses through key indicators (planning/presentation/assessment/student experience).

throughout the faculty needed thorough review to ensure that scarce resources were well directed in the future, and that promising innovation was well supported. Moreover, proven areas of existing strength should prepare for new, flexible conditions (including multimedia distance learning provision).

Research

In research, a force field of four more critical factors was identified (see Table 5.2). Again, the factors that activate change are widely recognizable. As higher levels of professional expertise grow throughout education, so will the demand increase for research, development and evaluation (B1), and for participation in these. As faculties of education compete to meet diverse research needs, they will see advantage in developing distinctive areas of research expertise (B2). Where an active research climate has grown, individual teams and individuals within the faculty will be motivated to join it (B3). Finally, and in order to survive, faculties of education will need to meet pressures from their own universities to build centres of research (B4). Other faculties may recognize, to a lesser or greater degree, the forces resisting this faculty's development, and its plan of action. It had to acknowledge that it was building from a modest base; it still has far to go.

General faculty issues

Finally, the faculty identified four general factors which may activate (or resist) change (see Table 5.3). Through the new structure the faculty aimed to create a climate of learning teams (C1), synergized by staff who have the confidence, nimbleness and clarity of purpose to enact best thinking (C2). It placed many hopes on the promised new building, though it was acknowledged that a true integration of vision, values and enactment in the faculty depended essentially on the people who share in its work. Meanwhile, it faced serious constraints such as cultural resistance; an ageing staff; financial constraints, and uncertainty about government policy on student recruitment. The actions that the faculty proposed were only a beginning.

Table 5.2 Research: critical factors and action plan

Force field of critical factors		Action plan
Activating development	*Resisting development*	
B1 *Increasing professional demand for educational research* Especially school based and school focused research.	More competition for limited research funds.	Co-ordinate funded research bids; provide support for active/successful bidders.
B2 *Pressure to identify and support recognized areas of research*	Not good policy to neglect other worthwhile areas; need to create a widely shared research community.	Target resources at identified groups. Establish 3–4 focused research groups/ chapters (eg language/literacy; policy and administration; curriculum development; special needs).
B3 *Resurgent activity/output among teams and individuals*	Fear of emerging research culture; lack of confidence in developing research skills.	Provide regular support/mentoring through a new Office for Educational Research; resource national/international quality research; increase research active staff.
B4 *Pressure to build regional/ national/international reputation in research*	Little room to manoeuvre on staffing policy until research inactive staff refocus or move on.	Second phase of staffing policy will include seeking sponsored posts in established/ resurgent research areas; identifying new research posts; making 'adjunct' senior appointments/invitations to visit.

Table 5.3 General faculty issues: critical factors and action plan

Force field of critical factors		Action plan
Activating development	Resisting development	
C1 Emergent teams in research and new teaching modes	Old structures; cultural resistance; scarce discretionary funds to support new ventures.	Restructure the faculty two tier, teams based arrangements.
C2 Flexible, creative staff (in research, in teaching, and in collegial commitment).	Ageing staff; overproportion of tenured staff.	Staffing policy included voluntary early retirement (tax enhanced); promotions rather than tenure; offer longer contracts where appropriate. In anticipation of more flexible industrial legislation, work towards 'teaching only' loads, where appropriate.
C3 Relocation of faculty in one building	Financial constraints on university may delay construction.	Work to enhance inter-college communications; keep relocation on the university agenda.
C4 Devolved funding allows choice in pressure to achieve a balanced budget.	Constraints in government funded recruitment; need to meet recruitment targets; need to motivate staff, or help them move on.	Develop diversity in teaching; develop main areas of research, and target funding there; reduce staff levels in order to prepare for fresh recruitment in new areas.

Postscript

Writing on the impact of postmodernist thought in education, Ball (1994: 10) suggested that 'policies are always incomplete in so far as they relate to or move on to the 'wild profusion' of local practice. Policies are crude and simple. Practice is sophisticated, contingent, complex and subtle'. There are, indeed, real tensions between framing policy and enacting practice. Planning policy requires clear intelligence, hard work and willingness to attend to detail. Day to day practice, though, requires more elusive qualities of intelligence – namely, of emotional intelligence. To illustrate the delicate interstices that make up the web of actual practice, an extract follows from the (taped) working journal of the faculty dean:

> Nearly eight in the morning, still quiet here. Again, my programme looks too 'busy' today. Emergency meeting of deans, on budgeting; four individual colleagues and three staff deputations to meet; school visit; lunchtime international programme seminar; research consultation . . . not unlike yesterday. But yesterday's programme doesn't mention Joan's awkward warnings about delayed computer provision; nor Keith's distress, during our low-key (as I had thought) discussion on early retirement; nor Tony's much greater distress about the ending of his contract; nor my frustration at delays in getting quality issues into place in teaching programmes . . . This time yesterday I was reviewing Esmeralda's paper for the Toronto Conference (Brodeth 1997). She wrote of the good leader's 'capacity to listen, to be open to the "truths" of others – to accept what I may not want to hear . . .' Hmmm, not easy, but will try.

Lingard (1996: 69) claimed that the work of critical policy analysts should be 'underpinned by a commitment to greater justice, equality and freedom', although actual policy makers operate in what post-structuralism defines as a knowledge/power axis. In endorsing Ball's thesis (1994: 10) that policy is an 'economy of power', Lingard (1996: 72–3) emphasized the essential moral dimension (justice, equality, freedom) to which policy theorists, makers and practitioners must all contribute. Without this dimension, self-management is reduced to the Benthamite 'panopticon of modern educational organization' and self-management becomes a 'mechanism for delivering reform' (Ball 1994: 72).

This, as Lingard acknowledges (1996: 86), is certainly a modern problem, and a commitment to uncertainty also reflects the manufactured uncertainty of the present era. However, this uncertainty has surely existed in all times and all areas of human leadership; it is not confined to modern times, nor to postmodernist conditions. Faculty leaders must ensure that they take action to bring about needed change; yet, in the final course, and to quote the familiar song, 'it ain't what you do, but the way that you do it'. To qualify that, and to ensure that means and ends continue to justify each other, they must always work *within* a framework of decent respect for justice, equality and freedom, in order to achieve those ideals through educational policy and practice. Humane action needs clear thinking; and clear thinking needs humane action, in order to achieve the kinds of changes that will benefit *all* in the community who are served by the university.

6

INVESTING IN PEOPLE:

INVESTING IN SYSTEMS

Before the Education Reform Act 1988, few schools in the UK had any kind of formal development or strategic plan and little control over their finances. The majority of funding for education was, as now, determined by central government policies but the local education authorities (LEAs) had responsibility for the way educational spending was allocated for schools and colleges in their area. LEAs therefore had extensive powers, including control over staffing levels. Governing bodies, which generally had a majority representation of LEA officers and elected members, could, and sometimes did exercise a variety of controls but their powers were limited. However, as Gray (1984) made clear, in the early 1980s, once allocations had been made,

> important decisions concerning the allocation and deployment of these staffing and financial resources [were], by and large, left to those within the schools and colleges – and remarkably little [was] known about the ways in which such decisions [were] arrived at, the criteria used in making them, or the impact and outcomes of the selected forms of deployment in terms of the education of the nation's pupils and students.
>
> (Gray 1984: 209–10)

As we discussed in Chapter 1, post-1988, many things changed. The government of the day was determined that educational standards should be raised, achievements measured and management made more efficient. Weary teachers began to feel that pretty well anything which could conceivably be measured, had to be measured. Training and the achievement of national standards were considered to be necessary in order to improve not only schools and colleges, but also industry and commerce.

Numerous training initiatives were introduced by the then Department of Education and Science and the Employment Department, now merged into the Department for Education and Employment (DfEE), often in partnership with other organizations. One such initiative was the Investors in People (IIP) programme, which was first launched in the UK in November 1990 and funded via the Training and Enterprise Councils (TECs) in England and Wales and the Local Enterprise Companies (LECs) in Scotland. The aim was 'to encourage effective training and development within organisations, in line with business goals – and to acknowledge this commitment with a nationally recognised award' (Employee Development Bulletin 1992: 16).

So, the success or otherwise of the training had to be measured, assessed and a national award, the IIP 'standard', given to those who 'passed'. It was not enough to achieve the minimum levels of attainment and then for ever claim the IIP standard, use the IIP logo and fly the IIP flag. Every three years, the organization's record had to be reassessed in order to ensure that the standards had not slipped. The fact that the training and development had to be 'in line with business goals' ensured that any plan for staff updating and development had to be integral to the organization's strategic plan. In some ways, that was helpful to hard pressed human resource (HR) managers who were frequently in the position of having to fight their corner for funds against powerful departmental barons. One management consultant, Richard Finn, considered that the IIP programme

> struck exactly the right note as management gurus around the world were exhorting employers to introduce 'continuous improvement' and develop 'learning organisations' because employees were the 'only long-term sustainable competitive advantage'.
>
> (Finn 1994: 31)

Some employees might perhaps have balked at being designated as a 'competitive advantage', but at least the Investors programme was giving them front line consideration – in some cases for the first time in their working experience. Finn felt that 'there was something in the standard for most of the stakeholders':

Chief executives like the standard because it gives them a high profile in human resource activities and enables them to focus their business plan on and for staff; HR directors like Investors in People because it provides them with an external benchmark for their activities, and helps justify expenditure; employees like the standard because it gives them real development opportunities and an employer to be proud of; TECs like it because it gives them a framework for a strategy for the employed in their area, and an entry mechanism to local employers; academics like it because the standard is, in principle, an excellent model of human resource development; and finally, consultants like it because it has brought them lots of work!

(Finn 1994: 31)

At first, IIP developed slowly. Achievement of the standard demanded a major commitment and probably hard pressed industrial concerns felt that they had enough to cope with without putting themselves through unnecessary hoops. However, interest has begun to increase. Moreover, numbers of schools and colleges have now recognized that the IIP framework can help in formalizing their own staff development programme and ensuring that it forms an integral part of strategic planning. It is, after all, a perfectly sound and straightforward management structure to which educational institutions can relate.

The standard

The standard incorporates four key principles, linked to twenty-three performance indicators.

It is described in the *Industrial Relations Review and Report* of 1992 as follows:

The aim is that IIP should be relevant to all organisations and will be flexible enough to take account of different approaches to developing people. The key principles of the standard are that an Investor in People:

- makes a public *commitment* from the top to develop all employees to achieve its business objectives;

- regularly *reviews* the training and development needs of all employees;
- takes *action* to train and develop individuals on recruitment, and throughout their employment; and
- *evaluates* the investment in training and development to assess achievement and improve future effectiveness.

(Employee Development Bulletin 1992: 16)

Since its original publication, the standard has remained the same, though some of the terminology has been slightly changed in order to 'simplify the language of the standard and make it more consistent' (IIP 1996) and to reinforce the message of continuous improvement.

DfEE support for Investors

The DfEE (1997) clearly sees the relevance of Investors to schools, though their advice relates equally well to colleges. The introduction to *Investors in People and School Self-Improvement* reminds readers that

> Successful schools are learning organisations which value pupil achievement and staff development. They have a unity and clarity of purpose – a vision, and targets towards which everyone is working.
>
> Such schools recognise that there will always be areas where they and their pupils can do better. They put into practice a cycle of self-improvement which focuses on pupil progress and achievement. They know that improvement can only be continuous and sustained if everyone is involved in reviewing practice, deciding what needs to be done and making sure that change is managed systematically. They recognise the central importance of investing in staff development and training to ensure that the best possible education is delivered in the classroom.

(DfEE 1997: 1)

The introduction continues by advising that

> Investors in People can help schools to meet the development and training needs of everyone who plays a part in the success

of schools – from the governing body to voluntary helpers. It shows how working towards the Investors in People Standard complements school self-improvement and can play a part in raising standards of pupil performance.

(DfEE 1997: 1)

The emphasis throughout is on pupil achievement, which, it is suggested can be exemplified by schools asking

- How well are we doing?
- How do we compare with other schools?
- What more should we aim to achieve this year?
- What must we do to make it happen?

That sounds reasonable enough, and many institutions will have asked themselves similar questions in preparation for the self-assessment or self-evaluation of their work. So why is Investors in People so different? It could be that if the government had not introduced requirements for formal planning, accountability and demands for improved efficiency, schools and colleges would just have carried on in the same way as before, with the vast majority of committed teachers doing an excellent job, the very small minority of slackers giving students short shrift and managers doing their best in difficult circumstances. No more. The new regime has required educators to examine their practices, identify gaps, set targets for the improvement of student performance and then to be judged *against national standards*. Senior managers have been required to attend courses and seminars in order to learn how to manage, and in September 1997, the new National Professional Qualification for Headship (NPQH) was launched. The publicity for the NPQH indicated that training was to be focused, once again, on meeting national standards, but this time in five key areas:

- strategic direction and development of the school
- learning and teaching in the school
- people and relationships
- development and deployment of people and resources, and
- accountability for the efficiency and effectiveness of the school

(Teacher Training Agency 1997)

The terminology may be slightly different, but the spirit is very similar to that of the Investors initiative. Both these programmes require far more than just tinkering with existing systems and practices. They involve a full scale audit of current practice, against national standards.

It is easy to dismiss tinkering as a futile waste of time, but on some occasions, it may be helpful in dealing quickly with a particular problem. There is little point in refusing to put out a fire in the kitchen because the entire house requires a full scale restructuring plan. It might be advisable first to put out the fire, identify what caused it and then start work on the plan. Kanter (1989), writing about change in US business practices, partly commends what she describes as 'fine tuning', but she is right in questioning whether that will be enough to achieve fundamental change. She writes:

> Among the most promising 'themes' adopted by businesses to encourage incremental innovation are the concepts of 'total quality' and 'continuous improvement' – both predicated on the assumption that continual striving to reach higher and higher standards in every part of the business will provide a series of small wins that add up to superior performance. Such efforts point in the right direction – toward organizations able to learn and adapt to the demands of a rapidly changing business environment. But is 'continuous improvement' enough, or are more dramatic changes in structure and systems and sensibilities required? The pressures that businesses face today suggest that more than fine-tuning is in order.
>
> (Kanter 1989: 10)

The pressures which have faced teachers and education managers can hardly have been less than those faced by businesses. However, without good people, neither tinkering nor fundamental restructuring will work. People *are* the organization and the heart of the Investors initiative lies in the development of people in ways which enable them *to do their jobs well*. That is surely as much a requirement for education as for business.

So does it work?

Is it really worth all the time, trouble and cost to businesses or to education in actually working towards final assessment? The survey into attitudes of employers to Investors in People, carried out after the first three years of operation (Spilsbury and Stone 1995; Spilsbury *et al.* 1994) discovered that

- in over 66 per cent of participating companies, it had changed their training practices
- commitment to training had improved and the quality and quantity of training had increased
- overall, 57 per cent of employers believed that involvement with Investors had improved the quality of the workforce
- a more formally structured approach to training delivery had generally been achieved in participating companies
- employers involved in Investors had a more formal structured approach to training delivery.

(Spilsbury and Stone 1995: 415)

All very positive gains, but the researchers were obliged to say that 'a final link between involvement with Investors and improved business performance is yet to be made' (Spilsbury and Stone 1995: 418). That is not surprising. They conclude that

> it is difficult to establish whether it is involvement with Investors which encourages employers to develop the above characteristics or whether it is employers who already have the characteristics who are attracted to the initiative. It is also hard to establish whether this increased formalisation of employer policies and practices has actually led to a 'bottom line' improvement. This is because so many different factors affect business.

Adams (1996: 11), writing about the impact of Investors on businesses, reminds us that the rationale for Investors has always been 'to achieve hard-nosed objectives like increased profitability and efficiency by improving training', but she agrees that, 'unfortunately, such links are notoriously hard to prove'. Quite so, and if they are hard to prove in business organizations, how much harder will they be in education, which is not in the business of measuring output in terms of widgets produced per hour or percentage increase in profits per year. We are in the long term business of developing students' potential, and some of the outcomes may well take a very long time to come to the surface. However, once government money has been allocated to a new initiative, ministers will inevitably, and not unreasonably, be looking for positive evidence of returns on their investment. After all, they are spending taxpayers' money. Perhaps it should be enough to say that Investors may well have made a contribution to improvement in performance, though those who pay the piper are rarely satisfied if the tune is not quite to their liking.

The increase in the number of participating schools and colleges

Though it is not exactly a landslide, increasing numbers of schools and colleges are nevertheless now participating in Investors. But questions still remain as to why. Not all institutions are interested and they continue to survive. Headteachers, principals and teachers are experienced enough in providing staff development programmes, and over the years, government money has been regularly provided to enable such programmes to be offered. Why could they not just devise their own staff development framework and strategy, custom built for their own requirements? At a time when they were required to jump through so many hoops at the insistence of government, why volunteer to jump through even more? Accurate information is difficult to obtain about the numbers of institutions who are or were involved, including those who have achieved recognition, those who are in the process of working towards the final assessment and those who dropped out, but discussions with TEC advisers makes it clear that in certain areas at least, numbers are increasing significantly.

The DfEE has now given full support to the Investors initiative, by publishing the *Investors in People and School Self-Improvement* booklet. Included in this booklet is an example of one school's approach to achieving improvements in practice. The school recognized that it needed to improve reading standards and so set targets for raised performance. The headteacher realized that in order to achieve those targets, 'teachers and classroom assistants needed to improve their practice in teaching reading. They also needed to introduce the new approach to governors'.

The whole-school programme was paced over two years, and was constructed to ensure that staff were supported in developing their skills through the following stages:

- An awareness raising session was held for all staff and governors.
- The LEA English adviser was involved throughout the two year period, to advise and monitor progress.
- Two staff attended a five day skills development course spread over one term (Term 1). These two staff put the ideas learned into practice, and met regularly to share and assess experience (Term 2). In Term 3 they cascaded their experience to all staff using two INSET days.
- The headteacher increased her teaching load to enable other teachers to monitor and observe colleagues in action.

- As the techniques spread in the school, weekly and later monthly after-school meetings were used to compare and share experiences (Term 4).
- All teachers monitored their own progress by using a skills checklist and by observing more experienced colleagues.
- A staff development review took place every half term, and staff set new personal learning objectives.
- Continuous monitoring of pupil development in reading was carried out using National Curriculum attainment targets.

This carefully planned approach led to all staff being skilled and confident teachers of reading. Internal evaluation showed that pupils' reading was improving. Pupils' interpersonal skills also improved and this led to better pupil behaviour (DfEE 1997: 13).

This would appear to be a sound approach to dealing with an identified problem. The action taken involved target setting, monitoring, sharing of experience, formal staff development reviews, continuous monitoring of pupil development in reading and, in the light of findings, adjustment of learning objectives. Would all this have happened without Investors? Who knows? Discussions with former primary HMI and LEA advisers recalled examples of very similar approaches to the resolution of problems in some schools well before the Investors strategy was introduced. Good schools, they claimed, would always have operated in this way, though they might not have recorded every stage of the operation. However, there is little doubt that not all did, and conversations with the staff of some of the schools which had achieved IIP recognition had little doubt that in their view, the programme had helped them significantly to get their house in order in numerous ways.

The headteacher of Standish Community High School in Wigan, the first secondary school to achieve recognition (in 1993), was certainly convinced. The Education Reform Act 1988 had stimulated him, and the senior management team, to take stock of the school's position, and it was discovered that all was not well.

- School performance and quality were not monitored.
- The school had reached a plateau and needed to move forward with new vigour. .
- Training of the teaching staff was ad-hoc and often related to individual preference.
- Attitudes to non-teaching staff were outdated and their expectations were low.

(IIP 1995: 117)

It was clear that something had to be done to improve the situation. Although the business language appeared formidable, it was eventually decided to commit the school and its staff to the Investors in People programme. It was seen as 'a common sense method of managing a school in the 1990s'.

The journey to achieving recognition was daunting.

• An initial staff survey was carried out to establish the position against the Standard. There was concern when it revealed that no one could describe the role of the school, nor their role within it.
• The head took on the role of team leader and established a multi-discipline project team.
• An early task for a group of selected staff was to draft a mission statement, followed by core aims for the school and staff.

They had some way to go, but gradually, and progressively, the team was able to introduce

• team briefing which covered all staff
• clear roles and responsibilities for all which included line managers having responsibility for managing the development of their staff
• a Training and Development Policy Statement
• training needs analysis through development appraisal for all staff, effective induction for all new recruits.

(IIP 1995: 188)

A good many benefits of participation in Investors in People were claimed, including a change in school culture; more flexible working practices with both teaching and non-teaching staff; a greater understanding of the importance of quality and pupil care; more focused training, not only on the needs of the individual, but also on the needs of the school and, of even greater importance, improved pupil examination grades; an increase in 'staying on' rates; a large increase in the number of pupils applying to come to the school and a reduction in absenteeism.

Impressive claims, but is it possible that all the credit can go to the Investors programme, or would the school have shaken itself up after the 1988 reforms in any case? Who knows? Certainly IIP and the support of the TECs enabled work to start on blowing away many of the school's cobwebs and establishing an entirely different way of working.

Similar satisfaction was reported by Endike Primary School in Hull, which, after recognition in 1993, claimed that

> the school developed closer links with community, parents, governors, local businesses and agencies. The school ethos focused on involvement, teamwork and staff development. Successes have included:
>
> - no cuts in training budget
> - unauthorised absence rate well below 0.5%
> - disciplinary incidents and accidents reduced by 50%
> - attendance rates up from 70% to well over 90%
>
> (DfEE 1997: 24)

Though these improvements definitely took place, it is as hard to attribute them all to the Investors initiative as it was to prove that it had been responsible for many of the changes in industrial and commercial concerns. Perhaps it should be enough just to note the changes with admiration and to assume that IIP could well have contributed to the victory.

So, overall, schools which achieved the standard seem to be pleased they decided to accept the challenge. Moreover, in the case of those who achieved early recognition, most have shown they are willing to go through the whole process again in order to prepare for re-recognition. But what about colleges, which are generally much bigger, with far more complex structures than schools? Why did they decide to participate?

The college perception

Discussions with a number of college managers produced a variety of answers, but in the majority of cases the responses followed the lines of

> Investors imposed a discipline on us, and a structure. With all the demands on us at present, without Investors, the timetable would inevitably have slipped. There would always have been other more urgent jobs to do. We had outstanding advice and guidance from the TEC assessors, most of which cost us very little. We were not skilled at planning and monitoring performance, and we were able to learn numerous skills within the IIP structure.

We already had what I think was a really good staff development programme, but it was not planned or delivered systematically. Moreover, although workshops and courses were provided to help staff to cope with new assessment techniques and new programmes, it was all a bit ad hoc. It was, I'm afraid, too often on the lines of crisis training to cope with a problem and to survive for another day. Now, we have to try at least to anticipate what's coming and what staff will need to be able to do to do the job well.

We did not have appropriate structures in place. The college is large and on six different sites and we knew we had to find better ways of managing. Something had to be done. We were approached by the TEC about committing ourselves to the Investors initiative, and once we had thought seriously about what would be involved and by when, we were confident we should commit ourselves.

We wanted a national standard. We wanted people to know we had measured up and could be compared with the best. Many of our courses are linked to businesses in the area, either for work placements or for providing jobs for our students once they have qualified. We decided we needed the Investors standard to demonstrate we were good enough. We needed to be sure local employers would support us.

One personnel officer of a very large college reported that

Investors was considered to be a 'good thing' in principle as an aid to getting our systems and structures in line, and it did, though it took some time. When we had the first assessment, we didn't have the systems in place. The TEC adviser helped us to set that right.

This college's involvement with Investors in People coincided with a turbulent period brought about by imposed contract changes, which resulted in ongoing disputes and 'works to rule'. At that time, any attempts to introduce appraisal or restructuring schemes were resisted. However, if progress were to be made in the Investors process, some form of appraisal was clearly going to be necessary in order to find out exactly what people did in the college and formally to identify training and development needs. It might be said that management should have known what everybody did, and certainly teaching timetables were well documented. But staff of the college did a great deal more than teach. It was only when relative calm was restored and an uneasy contractual truce was more or less agreed that it became possible to introduce a 'development review scheme'. The term 'appraisal' remained unacceptable for some time.

Everyone interviewed in the colleges made the particular point that formerly, although in many cases good staff development programmes already existed, they were invariably for teachers. Investors required all employees to be included. In some colleges, the support group outnumbered the rest, and their inclusion in training and development programmes changed the entire culture of the college. What was perhaps more significant was the fact that working towards the standard required a strengthening of the line management structure. As one senior member of staff commented,

> Investors changed the management process. It made line managers act like managers and it crystallized the management role at different levels. Responsibilities were made clear. There was no backing off.

This view was strongly supported by the director of curriculum planning in another college, but she also considered it was important that managers had to meet individual members of their staff on a one to one basis. Everybody was entitled to meet their line manager and to discuss needs as they related to their job, and these meetings had to be recorded.

In another college, clarification of the role and responsibilities of team and curriculum leaders contributed significantly to the arduous task of producing the strategic plan, to the extent that team and curriculum requirements were clarified and carefully thought-out requirements recorded. Staff training and development became part of the plan.

> Team leaders quickly learnt that they have a lot of responsibility for the working lives of the people in their team. It was no longer enough to say 'I know what is needed, so there's no need to go through all this performance'. They have to provide evidence that they have discussed what is needed for the work of the team and why. They have to justify their recommendations.

The problems of effective communication in large colleges were frequently aired, and all were searching for the ultimate solution to information overload. They are not alone. It is unlikely that an organization exists which does not include small or large numbers of people who on occasions claim that 'Nobody Ever Tells Me Anything' – the NETMA condition reported in Chapter 2. However, colleges did feel that Investors had helped communication in a good many ways. At the very least, it had forced senior managers to talk to the people with whom they worked and just talking and listening to each other was a move in the right direction.

The answer to all our problems?

So, has the Investors in People programme been an unconditional success in every case? That would probably be too much to hope for. Senior managers we spoke to were, in almost every case, convinced of the help the initiative had provided, and (as a side benefit), participation appeared to have done a great deal to help schools and colleges to do well in Office for Standards in Education (Ofsted) and Further Education Funding Council (FEFC) inspections. As one headteacher said, 'it takes the sort of shake-up Investors gives you to know what your weaknesses are, and that gave us the opportunity to sort out our problems before the inspection team did it for us – *and* published their report for the world to see.'

Some of the conscripted participants were less convinced. They complained of meetings fatigue, more and more demands for information and for evidence of everything under the sun. Several felt strongly that going for the standard was just something to give the headteacher or principal more brownie points. 'We could have told him what was wrong and what needed to be set right without all this disruption'.

One senior manager felt that the name Investors in People gave a wrong idea of what it was all about, namely, among other things, to produce a structure and a staff development programme designed to help people to perform well in the interests of the organization. Some people, she had discovered, were disillusioned because they felt, as individuals, they had merely been pawns in the larger game. One teacher said 'this college has done nothing for me as a person, only as a cog in the college wheel.' In that particular case, her judgement proved to be unjust, but similar feelings were expressed equally strongly by a number of valued people in many other colleges. The work involved in achieving recognition was, as everyone acknowledged, formidable. One of the major tasks was the production of the portfolio of evidence, which involved cross-referencing.

Gathering the evidence together was a major task in itself, but the cross-referencing made the job wearisome.

No initiative will be capable of solving all our problems. All that can be said is that senior staff of those institutions which succeeded in achieving the standard appear to be convinced of its value; that they learnt a great deal and that, if nothing else, it enabled a thorough overhaul of systems and procedures to take place. 'Yes', said one disgruntled forced participant. 'It's done that, but it would have been better to call it Investors in Systems rather than Investors in People. It's just another management tool which uses people (that's us) as fodder'.

Those who have not yet been persuaded of its value would no doubt say they already do all the things Investors require, or that they already have too much to do and can't take on one more major job. The views of schools and colleges who started but then dropped out are more difficult to ascertain.

The final word?

The comment volunteered by a mature student in a college lunch queue might perhaps serve as a postscript. She was asked if she knew anything about the Investors programme. She did, because she had been interviewed by an IIP assessor, and reports on progress had regularly been included in the college newsletter. Had she seen any signs of changes brought about by the programme? She replied, 'Well, this college was in chaos at one time. Now, things seem to work. Did Investors in People do that? If so, good. It was all hopeless before. Things got lost or not done – or done twice'.

What about the people who worked in the college? Had things improved for them? She hesitated before answering, but then said, 'I can't say. I don't know enough about how they regard their work here, but if the administration is working more smoothly, it must be even better for the staff than it is for us. Think of all the hassle they must have had to put up with before.'

7

CONTROLLING? OR CONNECTING? WORKING TOGETHER TO FIND SOLUTIONS

This chapter draws on observations of educators as they interact with other people in order to do their daily work. It provides examples from tertiary settings, in order to look at ways in which the rhetoric and good resolutions of management are put to the test in day to day encounters. The chapter shows that it is only through such encounters that important skills in mediation – such as leading by personal example; being slow to anger, but unafraid to confront; tackling issues, not personalities; requiring a continuity of interaction, beyond the resolution of any single issue – can be truly tested.

The International Institute of Negotiation and Conflict Management (IINCM) was founded in 1996 to serve industrial, commercial, professional and academic organizations. In its quarterly newsletter *Inter-Act!*, Kenfield (1997: 2) acknowledged that, in a 'fast-changing world, with its limitless challenges and endless conflicts, there is a great, unsatisfied demand for the knowledge and experience accumulated in the old/new field of conflict management'. At the organizational level, it is clear that the need for such an institute has emerged, not least through the extremely high costs that can be incurred through traditional groups of adversarial litigation, which continues to be an immensely larger business than conflict management and dispute resolution.

The importance of mediation through negotiation, rather than conflict through litigation, applies to individuals just as it does to organizations. The scope for mediation skills is not confined to formal disputes, which may or may not involve the law. Rather, the consciously learned techniques of listening, consulting, negotiating and resolving should become second nature for professionals and managers, so that expertise in mediation operates in continuous, reliable and unconscious harmony with the creative pursuit to get things done.

As Pepper (1995: 91–2) pointed out, this view is not new to best organizational management theory and practice. Pepper records that Mary Parker Follett (1868–1933), whose business philosophy was well ahead of her time, identified three methods for dealing with conflict: domination, compromise and integration. Her view was that only integration can work, since 'orders should flow naturally out of the situation in which the order giver and receiver find themselves. The orders should not be seen as the whim of the boss; rather, they should be seen as a by-product, a natural conclusion of a flow of events'. In order to achieve an integration of manager–worker interests, Follett argued, 'the participation of employees should take place before the order is given, not afterwards' (quoted in Pepper 1995: 92). She emphasized four aspects of coordination that lead to integration: coordination through agreement to come together; through working at the early stages of organizing; through understanding that coordination is reciprocal (involving adjustment not only to people, but also to issues), and through continuous further integration.

Yet leadership, as so many practitioners and theorists have declared, must above all be decisive. Is there time, in a busy educator-manager's life, always to go through this cycle of consultation and coordinated interaction? The answer, we suggest, lies in understanding that it is only through interaction that the synergies can happen to get things done. Consultation is not just the prelude to right action; rather it is right action itself. Similarly, the exercise of stability and of care in all human dealings is integral to sound management. It becomes clear, then, that a caring management is an efficient management; from this point of view, caring is a 'hard/tough' notion, not just a 'cosy/sympathetic' response. There is now, as Grogan (1997: 12) has shown, a body of successful practice and respectable theory, concerning the caring educator/administrator:

'when administrators see themselves as connecting with others instead of controlling others, the possibilities for collaboration and creative problem-solving increased dramatically'. She makes clear that care does not exclude the proper handling of conflict: 'when care replaces disgust, rage or indifference, the repair and mainten- ance of a relationship, now fragile, becomes possible' (Grogan 1997: 13). Such a version of caring involves, as Noddings (1995: 676) explains, 'a continuous search for competence', since it will be satisfied only with outcomes which satisfy the needs of both the organization and all the individuals involved in the interaction. These processes involve inevitable risks of frustration, wasted energy and failure to resolve issues. In this, the process is no different from all human dealings.

Interacting to get things done: the case of Ben

As the academic registrar of a large university science institute, Ben's professional workload is heavy, though he insists that he welcomes this, and enjoys working on the wide range of issues and problems that he encounters each day. He is one of those unusual people who welcome difficult financial tasks; can absorb and (more import- antly) interpret fine detail; prepare well composed reports and re- commendations, which move others towards well based decisions; and is willing to endure doubt rather than reach a too hasty con- clusion. He genuinely likes people and collaborating with them, and he shows his determination to continue to like people, even when they may behave less than likeably. He has high personal and pro- fessional standards, which can sometimes make him severe on others' sins of omission or commission, even though he continues to show patience with 'sinners as people'. Those high standards involve him in thorough probings of organizational slackness within and beyond the university, which may lead him to make under- standable strictures, for example, on the 'superficiality' of some highly placed senior colleagues who fail to maintain focus on issues, through failure to attempt to understand the 'whys?' which under- lie these.

Ben's working day is tightly organized. After dealing with e-mail, faxes, voicemail and snailmail (where no message is handled more than once, if at all possible), he briefs his senior assistant (who is in close harmony with his own working rhythms). As well as check- ing the morning's programme, they discuss a range of staff and resource relocations, before Ben begins his first appointment with the (all male) computer support team. Following a number of complaints from teaching, research and administrative staff about unexplained breakdowns, and failures to keep appointments to fulfil promises for action, Ben has called the team together in order to identify problems and take remedial action.

As each team member arrives, Ben greets them warmly, exchanges banter about winning and losing football teams and puts them at their ease. Once they are all assembled, he guides them beyond relaxed male clubbiness, to focus on why the meeting has been called – and to confront the need to get some rapid improvement in IT provision for the institute. Ben is well prepared for this meeting. He has organized the various complaints that he has received into clear agenda items, which include personal relations; budgeting/resources problems; and team leadership. After listening to responses from individual members, Ben concedes that institute staff cannot be expected always to behave perfectly, or even as well as the computer team might wish. He advises them on ways in which they can develop their own authority in handling, for example, staff who may be of high status, yet are often naive about computers, and who may seem to be wasting the team's time with trivial or elementary requests. Sometimes, these problems can be easily solved by an alert user, or even a beginner, who is willing to try to put things right before calling in a technician who might be on another campus site at that time.

'Okay,' says Ben, 'but before you get to the stage of thinking, "this guy is wasting my time," remember to keep focused on why you are there. If it is easy to put right, do it – and get them to follow what you do. If it is a more difficult problem, don't be tempted into giving them easy promises. Tell them when you *can* deliver, don't just say what you think they want to hear.'

Having dealt with a dozen such items during the twenty minutes' consultation, Ben sums up the various points of advice and agreement, and asks if all team members are happy now about putting them into action. They are, and this part of the meeting now closes. When all except the senior technician, Simon, have left the room, Ben continues discussion on a number of budget items. He then seeks Simon's view on a cluster of complaints that have risen, in particular, about Eric's allegedly off-hand 'rude' handling of people. These complaints have come from various parts of the institute. 'People are not happy with the computer service,' says Ben, 'and we have got to look for a change of behaviour here.'

Simon admits that Eric does not always communicate well. Ben asks how Eric behaves with Simon, and Simon answers, 'Well, I can control him but I cannot change his personality'.

'Is this a good enough answer?' asks Ben. 'Are you sure you're doing your work on his behalf, as his leader? If there is an attitude problem on your team, then don't you take some responsibility for this?' Discussion continues on this point for some minutes, as Ben probes sensitively, yet firmly, the need to accept an attitude problem as a team problem. He then passes on some commending reports from staff, on Simon's own personal success in sorting out technical problems and providing good support.

'Everyone says you're a really good technician, Simon. I am sure we made the right choice in appointing you to the post. I have a job to do, in supporting you to make sure that the "senior" bit of your title really works. So, for our sake, and for Eric's own sake, don't let him drift into a position where he is letting your team down. It's a work issue, not a "change of personality" issue.'

Simon agrees, eventually, that he will prepare his own advice to Eric, and the meeting ends on this good note of resolution. Five minutes later, the next meeting of the morning begins, with the institute architect. The institute is involved in a difficult process of relocating some laboratories and also some well established staff into another building. Few things are likely to stir emotions more than requirements on colleagues to relinquish space. Yet the institute, which is waiting for a long promised, purpose-built building, has been identified as occupying too much space in its present locations, compared to other higher education institutions.

Institute members are resisting attempts to 'squeeze' their space, as they wait for their new building. It is Ben's task to avert potential conflict here. The willingness of both Ben and Lorna, the architect, to see each other's point of view helps them to move swiftly to the substantive issues that need to be resolved. Gradually, towards the end of the meeting and having listened with care to Lorna's case, Ben offers advice on a less drastic, but just as useful solution to the space problem – and gets thanked by Lorna for doing so. The rest of the morning passes swiftly, in a flurry of phone consultations, report writing and discussions with his assistant. Throughout all these, Ben maintains a clear focus on each task. His high level of attention to detail, and his alertness to attitudes of people, are matched by a notably low level of emotional intensity. He is closely engaged, yet dispassionate; the intensive morning's work leaves him unstressed and looking forward to a well earned lunch break.

Later, reflecting 'from the balcony' (see Chapter 3) on his work, Ben discloses that, although he takes pride in ensuring that dialogue with all colleagues is friendly and constructive, he also relishes the element of having a 'good fight' in areas of conflict, when something has to be resolved. He knows that conflict must be managed, not avoided. The art, in his view, is to maintain a sense of purpose with all the tenacity that he can master, but never to let conflict become personal. Ben would, he said, 'die on the vine', if he could not draw on the commitment from both himself and his colleagues, whom he values as both allies and adversaries on different occasions. The institute provides a 'good environment' for creative administration, and is 'a good employer' – though he acknowledged that not all colleagues shared his views. He was glad that his work provided a diverse range of challenges on which to base different kinds of action. He thought of himself as being, at best, 'a good trader, willing to be flexible when necessary . . . in many senses we are in a business, and we should all understand the opportunities and constraints that this must involve'. Although he felt frustrated by some colleagues who 'can never move out of the mind set of saying "we have always done it this way, so we must continue to do it this way"', he had learned the importance of maintaining self-possession and of not allowing himself to become unduly upset by 'pet hates'.

A notable element, evident throughout observation of Ben's consultations and discussions, was his willingness to give just the same high quality of attention to the problems of a newly arrived junior technician that he would give to the university architect, executive dean or vice-chancellor. Ben is highly valued by senior colleagues for his skills in strategic planning, and for his ability to see the 'big picture'. Yet, in developing good 'balcony vision', he has not lost his unusual concern for those day-to-day particulars that can contribute crucially to the success or failure of an operation. It is fair to argue that senior leaders should never be distracted from attention to the larger picture, by becoming overpreoccupied with detail. It is also important, however, to acknowledge that the larger picture can be composed only of countless smaller details, all of which require appropriate attention.

In commending the good uses of having a 'good fight' in order to challenge each others' thinking, Eisenhardt *et al.* (1997: 78) declare that a crucial art in managing conflict is 'to encourage management teams to argue without destroying their ability to work together'. Following ten years of research on the interplay of conflict, politics, and speed in strategic decision making among management teams, Eisenhardt *et al.* made clear distinctions between teams which were successful or unsuccessful in avoiding interpersonal conflict. In teams which failed to avoid interpersonal conflict, individuals 'failed to cooperate, rarely talking with one another, tending to fragment into cliques, and openly displaying their frustration and anger'. It was common to hear individuals in these organizations described in terms such as 'manipulative', 'secretive', 'burned out' and 'political'. On the other hand, a team with minimal interpersonal conflict 'was able to separate substantive issues from those based on personalities'. Eisenhardt *et al.* (1997) identified six tactics that successful teams used for managing interpersonal conflict. Team members

- worked with more, rather than less, information and debated on the basis of facts
- developed multiple alternatives to enrich the level of debate
- shared commonly agreed goals
- injected humour into the decision process
- maintained a balanced power structure
- resolved issues without forcing a consensus.

(Eisenhardt *et al.* 1997: 78)

These tactics 'did not delay – and often accelerated – the point at which the team was able to make decisions'. Moreover, they found that the more information that managers can supply to their colleagues, the better the results – as long as the data are 'objective and up-to-date – since 'it encourages people to focus on issues, not personalities' (Eisenhardt *et al.* 1997: 79). This prospect of what Leonard and Straus (1997: 112) have termed 'creative abrasion' is clearly preferable to the 'comfortable clone syndrome', where everyone has been selected, then trained, to think alike. As is the case with Ben, a concern to provide accurate, useful information, combined with a relish for issues focused argument, and an enjoyment in collaborating (including arguing) with colleagues, provides an excellent recipe for achieving desired changes of direction.

Chan Kim and Mauborgne (1997: 65–6) have argued that the need for people to have their say is crucial in achieving fair process, and 'never has the idea of fair process been more important for managers than it is today. Fair process turns out to be a powerful management tool', which 'builds trust and unlocks ideas'.

Interacting to get things done: the case of Sarah

Sarah is head of a university business school, which operates on several campuses in the region. Having in mid-career established her reputation as a respected 'hands on' researcher and as a notably innovative and successful teacher, Sarah made a deliberate choice to take on duties in academic management, rather than just drift into it. Over a number of years she had accumulated an impressive range of experience on committee work, and was held in high esteem for her consultative, organizational and leadership qualities. Her view was that if the job had to be done, it must be worth doing well, and was likely to deserve the same quality of attention from her that she had always sought to give to her research and teaching.

Sarah's day begins early and pleasantly. She shares a morning coffee with her secretary, in the comfortable, civilized meeting space between her own small office and her secretary's working area. The flowers, table journals and informal seating arrangements provide a fine blend of welcoming domesticity with orderly working conditions. Sarah's discussions with her secretary Christine show her willingness to consult on issues – to explain and share, rather than direct, and Christine (who is senior in years to Sarah) is equally willing to offer her views on best ways to schedule a task, arrange a meeting, or respond to a problematic letter.

There is an aura of goodwill and quiet ease in Sarah's movements, tone of voice and day-to-day relations. When a senior colleague, Clive, telephones, she asks about his weekend family activities, gently teases him on these, and then addresses the issue that he raises with her. Finally, she asks him if she might borrow a text that she had noticed on his table during their last meeting. 'When would you like it?' he asks. 'Anytime,' says Sarah; three minutes later Clive appears with the text. Sarah has an ability to encourage people to do what she wants, though she is not manipulative. She gives them room to make their choice, and she is able to make people feel good by performing small acts of service.

The first meeting of the morning is with a mature postgraduate student, who has travelled some distance from a rural campus to Sarah's office. The student is seeking advice on course options. As is the case with all who have business with the head of the business school, Sarah establishes a sense of essential equality between them, through her easy, quiet, invitational style of questioning, which allows the student time to organize her thoughts and to tell her story in her own way. At first, the student is rather guarded, then discloses her criticisms of the way in which her questions and needs have been handled by a course tutor on the rural campus to which she is attached. Sarah shows that she has heard this criticism but does not probe further at this point. The student then talks about various pressures on her own life, which include caring for a young family and also working in a family business, while trying to gain her MBA. Gradually, Sarah moves from listening to explaining. Using her complete and detailed understanding of course programmes, she provides the student with some alternative options, and discusses each of these with her, allowing as many interventions and 'yes, buts' as the student wishes. Towards the end of the meeting Sarah hands the student a written summary of possible choices that she might make.

'You don't have to make your final choice now,' says Sarah. 'Think about it, talk about it at home or wherever, and let your tutor know what you have decided. I shall follow things up with him, to see what decisions you make.' 'That's great,' says the student, now distinctly happier and more relaxed.

When the student has left, Sarah asks Christine if she will make a note to raise at the next meeting of coordinating course tutors, about the need to ensure that students get appropriate support in making their course choices. 'I think we have got the right patterns for support in place now, don't you?' she says, 'but we may have to ask the tutors to be sure that the procedures are in actual operation now'. 'The student certainly had to come a long way to make her point,' agrees Christine.

Between this and the next meeting, Sarah telephones her administrative officer, to discuss the contents and completion date for a school report. She then welcomes Robin, one of her coordinating tutors. He wants to vary a course programme, which is still in the first weeks of being presented for the first time. Sarah listens to his reasons. There are, Robin explains, some discrepancies of course delivery between different campuses, and some tidying is needed. Sensing that there may be more to this than Robin has so far disclosed, Sarah asks why the need for change seems suddenly to have become urgent. Robin then explains that there has been some mounting student criticism about these discrepancies. The points of complaint include variation of teaching provision, student workloads and marking standards. Although Robin shows some discomfort in admitting this, Sarah's tact and encouragement enable him to make a full disclosure of the unease that has been expressed by students, and it is Robin himself who acknowledges that 'we should really have let you know about this some days ago'. 'Or weeks, perhaps?' intersperses Sarah, with mild, dry emphasis.

She adds that she is glad to know that Robin and his team wish to take remedial action, though she suggests too that the problem may not be confined to Robin's programme. This may be an issue that the whole school should confront as soon as possible, in order to meet the well justified complaints that students have been making. She observes: 'It's quite understandable, that students can get touchy about assessments and teaching provision'.

Robin agrees, and together they draw up a timetable for the achievement of common patterns of teaching and assessment across the campuses. Sarah also takes the opportunity to probe into a comparatively empty two-week period in the teaching timetable. She secures agreement with Robin that this period should provide an important opportunity to integrate academic components of the programme more effectively with actual professional business skills. Many of her colleagues, including Robin, she feels, need to be challenged in this respect, to make their course more professionally credible and useful. Robin undertakes to pass this advice onto his team and to consider ways and means of improving academic–professional links; the meeting then closes.

The remainder of Sarah's morning involves further meetings with individuals and groups of people. Throughout these she maintains an unhurried composure, which allows space to all those involved in the meetings. Just as important, she also achieves a remarkable economy in these processes. Because she is well prepared, there is a strong sense of forward direction, with few meanderings from main issues in the discussions. Frequently, we observed that she would be sure to take on tasks for herself, before asking others to take on a responsibility. In this way, colleagues were left with a sense that work was not only fairly allocated, but also shared. While she provided a careful summation of each meeting, she did not try to move too quickly to this stage, before colleagues could have their proper opportunity to contribute. Moreover, she ensured that colleagues were thanked and appreciated for making their contributions to meetings.

Reflecting on the events of the morning, and on wider aspects of her work, Sarah emphasized that she regarded herself, above all, as a 'facilitator and fixer' in these meetings. She very much enjoyed working in this way with colleagues; although she sometimes resented the reduced time available for her teaching and research, she had no doubt about the value of this kind of morning – 'as long as I can see that we are really getting somewhere with things that need to be done'. In negotiating with colleagues, Sarah preferred terms such as 'support' and 'facilitation', rather than 'contesting' or 'conflict management'. Where there was a risk of clashing on issues that might lead to interpersonal conflict, she preferred to 'turn away wrath', by injecting, for example, some humour into a discussion (her highly developed skills of irony and wit came into good use here).

For all her emphasis on the importance of consultations, Sarah disclosed that she also made a self-conscious effort to avoid 'over-consultativeness – I don't want to be wasteful with the lives of my colleagues, just as I don't want to waste my own time'. She reminded herself often that she wanted, above all, to 'lead by example', in achieving harmony through consultation: 'Of course, we often have to reach a decision that does not suit everybody, and sometimes not even a majority will be in favour. It is very important, at such times, that decisions must be seen to be well informed, even if they are not popular – that the decision has in a sense formed itself, out of the facts of the case.'

Consultations went wrong, she thought, when focus on the main issues is lost, through, for example, becoming overpreoccupied by minutiae, when people lose sight of the forest because of all the individual trees: 'If a meeting isn't well prepared, the people will always wander off into the trees,' she said. 'But I do believe that people really want useful meetings, they really want to see the school's record in teaching and research improve. I always feel an optimism – a guarded optimism, at least – that well run meetings do help the school to do all its work better. But it's not easy, getting the right balance between full consultation on the one hand, and clearing time to get things done, on the other.'

Sarah acknowledged that time had become a critical problem in her working week. This problem, as Moodie (1997: 42) has disclosed, afflicts many academics in management positions, who are less protected than most junior staff against unreasonable demands on their time. According to Moodie, managers 'get paid well enough not to have a claim for additional pay for overtime but they thereby lack a mechanism for protection against the intrusion of work into their personal lives'. Academic managers at Sarah's level are under intense pressure to give their time to subordinates, peers, seniors and people beyond the university. They have to attend a wide range of meetings arranged at all kinds of hours, social and non-social. Because they must be reliable role models, day-to-day, week-to-week and year-to-year, and appear as competent people who can be relied on to meet deadlines, many of which are imposed externally, their working days are often much longer than they would wish. Moreover, their work also spills into weekends and vacation times. As Moodie comments:

> We often say that managers who allow work to intrude heavily into their personal lives exploit themselves, but this is not how it appears to them. Declining an expectation to work late or finish a project during the weekend, compromises the very 'can do' quality that is important in securing their position. They perceive excessive work demands not as self-exploitation but as external impositions which are as intractable as standard hours of attendance are for their junior colleagues.
>
> (Moodie 1997: 42)

Just as middle managers are often caught between the needs of their subordinates and the expectations of their superiors, senior managers, too, 'often get confined to, if not trapped in, the expectations of their office'.

In Sarah's case, the long days and weekends that she has had to give to her work have been driven quite clearly by her concern that the school should be seen as a reliable provider of high quality teaching and research. When we were observing Sarah, it was tempting to surmise that – at least in the short term – she was in danger of becoming something of a victim of the perfectly justifiable drive to improve quality in tertiary education. However, her own view of this was that it is only through getting the 'quality message' home to every individual member of her staff, that her own heavy workload might be eased in the future. Meanwhile, she was still able to declare with some conviction that 'there is a huge amount to enjoy about my job – and as long as I can feel we are getting somewhere, then the extra hours and extra effort are well worth it'.

Achieving team synergy

In their influential text *Leading the Team Organization*, Tjosvold and Tjosvold (1991: 121) acknowledge that the way to achieving team synergy in pursuing common goals, cannot and probably should not always be easy: 'progress toward the team organization is a realistic, inspiring aspiration. Managers and employees can live with and often thrive upon difficulties and imperfections if they know where they want to go and believe they can get there . . . a problem-free life is neither realistic or desirable'. On the other hand, they point out, 'failure to make progress demoralizes managers and employees'. Discussing the right uses of task teams, Tjosvold and Tjosvold (1991: 126) provide an example of a team that needed to develop more cohesion, in order to become more efficient. It was decided to invite a colleague from another section of the organization, to act as the leader for a particular project. This colleague was familiar with their work area, but also had the advantage of being a cooperative outsider who brought the message that 'we can only be successful if we can empower each other'. Under her direction, the team devised the following provisional guidelines for themselves, as co-workers:

- our focus is on creating the best possible plan
- we all take credit; we all take responsibility
- we support each other inside and outside the group
- we treat each other with respect and listen to each other's ideas
- we show our confidence in each other
- we open-mindedly consider each other's ideas, and don't take disagreement as a personal attack
- when we have problems and frustrations with someone, we talk directly to that person or, if appropriate, bring it up at a group meeting
- gossiping and secret alliances are unacceptable.

(Tjosvold and Tjosvold 1991: 126)

Having established these self-disciplining do's and don'ts, the team was able to move rapidly in developing its project plan and, as the Tjosvolds made clear, this involves a good deal of spirited – but no longer personally acrimonious – disagreement.

In the successive stages of defining problems, creating solutions, examining alternatives and making decisions, Tjosvold and Tjosvold (1991: 136) emphasized the importance of achieving team consensus. This involves 'the most effective resolutions to important problems', although consensus is not usually appropriate for simple, unimportant issues, which can be resolved in less time-consuming ways. Although consensus cannot always be reached in its pure form of total agreement, it is important that due process allows all involved to say what they need to say, and for all others to listen to them. The Tjosvolds drew up seven basic rules for consensus decision making:

1 Express your own ideas clearly and logically, but avoid arguing blindly for them. Consider other viewpoints.
2 Change your mind based on the objective and logical arguments of others. Do not change your mind to avoid conflict.
3 Seek a consensus decision. Avoid majority voting, tossing a coin and bargaining.
4 Foster opposing views. Encourage people to become involved and speak their mind.
5 Discuss underlying assumptions and ideas. State the rationale behind your position.
6 Strive for a win-win solution that incorporates the best of all ideas. Avoid thinking in terms of winning and losing.
7 Reconsider an earlier decision. Sometimes a team should have a 'second chance' meeting in which team members express any remaining doubt and make changes so that they remain committed to the team solutions.

(Tjosvold and Tjosvold 1991: 136–7)

Linking this advice with the observations provided earlier, of Ben and Sarah as they were involved in their daily negotiations, we note that, in each of their cases, consultation and consensus were not ends in themselves, but simply a means of achieving higher standards and higher quality for their organizations. Discussing critical factors related to quality in higher education, Bell (1997: 38–9) drew on earlier quality models, including work by Parasuraman *et al.* (1990), to propose five dimensions of quality. These include *tangibles*, which require attention to such things as the physical facilities of a college, teaching course materials, and the personal presentation of staff. A second aspect of quality is *reliability*, which involves attention to consistency of performance of course delivery and assessment, systems and procedures. In the third area of *responsiveness*, the criteria include feedback and monitoring of courses and attention to student experience of the college. Then come aspects of *assurance*, which include staff academic credibility, reputation, competence, courtesy and the degree of security they can provide in the academic and social environment. Finally, quality needs to be demonstrated through *empathy*, which includes staff visibility, access and 'understanding the customer'. If managers wish to encourage the same high levels of concern for quality in customer service that Ben and Sarah have clearly pursued, they might be well advised to start – as was the case with Ben and with Sarah – by regarding the staff whom they manage as being the front line customers of their own management provision. Staff who are well treated by their managers (which does not mean being unduly favoured or over leniently treated), and who are genuinely involved in working together to find solutions, are themselves much more likely to be successful in their own handling of all the various clients – including students, colleagues and others – of the college.

Through observing the work of enlightened academic managers, we have discerned a sense of moral purpose in their dealings with colleagues, which is echoed in Kaku's (1997: 55) definition of the Japanese term *kyosei* (which can best be defined as 'a "spirit of cooperation", in which individuals and organizations live and work together for the common good'). *Kyosei*, suggests Kaku, 'can become a powerful force for social, political, and economic transformation'. For this reason, it should be at the heart of the business, or academic credo, and at the fingertips of a manager's daily operations.

8

THE QUIET WORKERS AND
THE TRUMPET BLOWERS

There have always been quiet workers and trumpet blowers in life. We have vivid memories of one departmental staff meeting where one of the quiet workers, weary of a colleague's seemingly never-ending accounts of his internationally renowned research, of his regular invitations to present keynote addresses at refereed conferences and his self-congratulation about numerous other achievements, said 'Excuse me Jim, but if you'd care to lend me your trumpet for a while, perhaps I can be given just the odd minute to put on record what the rest of us have been doing while you've been away for most of the year'. Enough was enough.

We have all met them. People who always make sure they send copies of letters or memoranda to important people in the organization which demonstrate how hard they are working or how brilliant they are, or both. People whose priorities will invariably be carefully constructed to ensure they achieve maximum personal enhancement. The quiet workers, the 'good old workhorses', as one of the trumpet blowers once described some of his colleagues, are often the people who just get on with their own work and leave their trumpets at home. The worst of this is, or can be, that leaders who have the power to recommend or withhold promotion are not always aware of precisely what workload some of these quiet workers carry, nor that some of them might feel they would like the occasional handful of oats to be thrown in their direction.

There is nothing wrong in being proud of achievements, nor of making them known. The problem is that the trumpet might play a sweeter tune if the mute were occasionally fixed. The introduction of appraisal or professional review schemes has to an extent helped to identify exactly what individuals do, but the form adopted for appraisal is variable. Unexpectedly, it has been three major, external initiatives, each of which, in different ways, has brought to light some of the previously unacknowledged achievements of quiet workers and, embarrassingly, the presence of skeletons in certain institutional and departmental cupboards. They are

- audits of quality assurance procedures in universities and in some colleges of higher education
- research assessment exercises
- quality assessment exercises.

The first to be considered relates to the audits of institutions' quality assurance processes and control systems.

Quality assurance audits

In the 1990s, it had become clear to university vice-chancellors and college of higher education principals that with a government on the rampage it would be as well to demonstrate that they were perfectly capable of monitoring practice in their own institutions. The Higher Education Quality Council (HEQC), funded by subscriptions from individual universities and colleges of higher education, took on the arduous task of carrying out audits of institutions' quality assurance systems and procedures. It was an in-house, not a government imposed, government funded initiative. Guidelines and checklists of good practice are drawn up by representatives of participating institutions and the HEQC 'invites' institutions to take part in an audit of their quality procedures. It might all seem rather cosy, but though the reports always take care to accentuate the positive, they also make it quite clear what needs to be done to rectify deficiencies. Reports invariably 'wish to commend' aspects of the university's or college's practice, but also 'invite' them 'to consider the advisability' or 'the desirability' of making numbers of changes and improvements.

The difference between 'advisability' and 'desirability' may seem to be slight, but, bland and courteous though the terminology is, institutions are quite clear what, in the opinion of the audit team, they do well and what they need to do better. We feel confident that senior staff of most institutions will consider the suggestions made by the team, but there is no *requirement* that they should take any action. The reports of visits are published and available for anyone to read, and so institutions will presumably wish to show themselves up in a good light, but if vice-chancellors disagree with the outcomes of the audit, they can no doubt ignore the suggestions for improvement and continue with their own practices.

Systems, not teaching

The visiting teams look at systems, processes and for evidence that these are being implemented. They do not look at teaching. This is considered to be a strength by some and a weakness by others. As one principal of an audited college which received some criticism said, 'You can have wonderful systems and still be doing a thoroughly bad job. Conversely, you can have really good teaching but inadequate systems. It's what happens in practice that matters.' Handy (1995), reminiscing about his experiences since he joined the staff of a business school 25 years earlier, reflected that

> At that time I thought that there was a science of management which, once it was known and taught, would solve all our problems. Now I know better. I know, for instance, that you can know everything that there is to know about business and still be a lousy manager.
>
> (Handy 1995: 191)

Quite true, though few people would claim that there is no need for theory *or* for formal procedures. As everyone knows, it is the application of systems which counts; it is only by walking around, observing, talking and listening that leaders can really find out what is going on. Problems arise when theory or systems in no way relate to or inform practice. Procedures, no matter how carefully devised, are useless if they only gather dust in a four inch wide folder with a fancy title on the spine, as we have seen in numbers of institutions. Some systems weary colleagues have even gone so far as to suggest to us that a too firm belief in systems and theory can actually get in the way of initiative and stifle innovation. Others have told us they are sick and utterly tired of being told how to do their job, as if there was ever only one way to do practically anything worthwhile.

The HEQC approach is certainly not on the lines of 'this is the way you should be doing things'. Quite the reverse. In *Guidelines on Quality Assurance* (HEQC 1994), for example, it is suggested that institutions might consider whether they have satisfactory responses to questions very similar to those proposed by the Investors in People initiative (reported in Chapter 6) namely:

- What are you trying to do?
- Why are you trying to do it?
- How are you doing it?
- Why are you doing it that way?
- Why do you think that is the best way of doing it?
- How do you know it works?
- How do you improve it?

(HEQC 1994: 3)

That seems to be a perfectly reasonable approach. Useful check-lists are provided in order to 'help those that may wish to compare their present arrangements with the guidance provided' (HEQC 1994: 45).

No one could really object to the contents of the checklists, which many institutions have found useful as reminders of what should really be covered in their quality framework. The following check-list, which relates to services and facilities for postgraduate research students, is typical:

Institutions of higher education will wish to have guidelines on postgraduate research students that are known to students and supervisors. These guidelines will normally include information on:

- procedures for the change of a supervisor
- grievance and appeals procedures
- details of training available for supervisors
- mechanisms for monitoring and ensuring that the various faculty and departmental arrangements for postgraduate research students are in accordance with policy.

And finally,

Institutions of higher education will wish to provide training for postgraduate research students appropriate to their needs.

(HEQC 1994: 51)

What could possibly be wrong with all that? Most universities now have a code of practice on the admission, supervision and examination of research students, and so that should be enough to ensure that all is well. However, discussions with students, careful reading of audit and assessment reports, and the findings of an investigation into barriers to completion of postgraduate research degrees provide stark evidence that the existence of a code of practice is no guarantee that it is implemented (Bell 1996). It is not admirably devised codes and procedures, but the way they are implemented that matters.

Universities have complained, in some cases bitterly, that they have been required to produce vast amounts of documentation for the HEQC audit teams, which took them away from doing essential work. There is no reward for doing well, nor are there punishments for doing badly, unless the audited institutions decide to take action themselves. So, some argue, why bother? However, it was the vice-chancellors and principals who not only supported the principle, but also provided the cash for the audits to take place. On balance, it must have seemed wise to keep smiling, do the paperwork and begin the process of collecting evidence.

Though the visiting audit teams take pains to speak to as many students and members of staff as possible, their time is limited, and inevitably only a small sample of people can be interviewed. As a rule, in spite of institutions' best efforts to inform everyone and to involve as many people as possible, the impact of the exercises on individuals must necessarily be limited. The same cannot be said about the following two initiatives, namely the research assessment and teaching quality assessment exercises, which require the participation of practically every member of the departments involved.

Research assessment exercises (RAEs)

UK universities had experienced four research assessment exercises up to 1996. Research has always been important in universities, so important in fact that chances of promotion without a good research profile are slim. Anecdotal reports abound of 'selfish' academics who put their own research well before any other responsibilities, such as teaching, administration or support for any postgraduate research students unfortunate enough to be allocated to them. There is little hard evidence that this state of affairs actually exists, possibly because the prospect of litigation by the alleged miscreants is sufficient to ensure that grumbles rarely reach the stage of public statements. In any case, prolific researchers are a valuable commodity in university departments and even if the allegations of selfish practice were to be proved, sins can sometimes be forgiven in the interests of departments' research ratings.

Research counts. High achievers in the research assessment exercises enjoy the prestige of public recognition and the respect of their peers. Departments can, and often do, use the acquisition of top grading as a marketing ploy. Universities which offer masters and doctoral programmes report that potential applicants are anxious to know how they fared in the last RAE, the assumption being that they prefer to be associated with a highly rated department. But the really valuable result of a high grade is that successful departments can generally look forward to the prospect of increased research funding. That has not always materialized. Funding to support research, granted as a consequence of RAE ratings comes to universities, not departments, and it is up to individual universities to decide how it should be allocated. One 'old' university department, which joyfully looked forward to a replenishment of its research coffers, was told that there would be no extra money, but had they not achieved the top grade, their departmental budget would have been cut more sharply.

Long before the RAE was ever thought of, academic staff were always urged to produce research which could figure in the institutional annual report (so that the research pecking order could be clear for all to see in the university), and which would enhance the reputation of the department and the university in a wider sphere through the publication of research in reputable journals.

There is nothing new about that – at least, not in the long established universities. In the past, the 'new' universities – former polytechnics and certain colleges of higher education – tended to have less of a research commitment. They had and still do have other priorities, but now, many are doing their utmost to establish a research culture and some are beginning to climb the research rating ladder.

The RAEs made departments' research performance public. All universities knew who had achieved what because the league tables were published. Vice-chancellors were alleged to call departments to order which had other than an excellent research record and to make threatening noises about budget cuts if they fell below the expected standards. We know of departments which fixed posters in strategic positions announcing 'We are a 5-star department'.

And why not? It is a considerable achievement, but the achievement of such a standard must necessarily have placed pressure on everyone involved. We even heard of people not sleeping the night before the announcements were made. On announcement day, champagne corks were said to have popped for the winners, leaving the losers to sink into despair and wait despondently for a call from the vice-chancellor.

The impact of the three RAEs

In our experience, pre-RAE, some academics just got on quietly with their research, and if they were not asked, they may not have bothered to mention what they were doing. However, a too individualistic approach to research could result in some unwelcome practice. For example, individuals who had won external research funding could nominate themselves as budget holders for research contracts. They could then behave almost as if they were in charge of their own housekeeping money. Budget holders who left to take up another appointment could take the budget with them to their new university, occasionally leaving research assistants and others high and dry. That sounds extraordinary now, but it happened.

The move to the management of research

The RAEs forced universities to formalize their research structure, to define more precisely what their research targets were, to identify who was research active, who was not, and what the non-research active were doing. *It made it necessary for research to be managed.* Research policies and plans were produced where few existed before. Particularly after the 1992 exercise, pro-vice-chancellors (research) were established in some universities. Research and researchers became orchestrated.

McNay (1997: 11) reporting on the outcomes of a project concerned with the impact of the 1992 RAE considered that it led to 'the further development of team based research and the decline of the "lone researcher".' It made it necessary for heads of department to find out and document just what research was being undertaken in their departments; to identify who was producing good research and who was not; to decide which type of research fitted into which criteria and which counted for most in the RAE game.

Of course, all this should have been normal practice, but the notion of academic autonomy, variously interpreted, at one time made it perfectly possible for individual activities to take place without anyone knowing, as happened in the case of one maverick individual researcher who submitted a research proposal to a major funding body with a colleague from another university. They were successful in their submission, but the individual concerned saw no reason to inform his university or his department and arranged that the funding would be paid direct to his colleague's university. He drew the equivalent of a salary from the fund while continuing to receive his own salary. He used his departmental research funds, secretarial and computer facilities, and then published under the name of his colleague's university.

The head of department discovered what had happened by attending the conference at which the outcomes of the research were presented. He was incensed, not least because he had himself submitted an application for the same project which had been unsuccessful. He quickly put into place a funnel structure which required every individual and every team to obtain clearance before forwarding applications for research funding. That in turn infuriated everyone else in the department, who complained that the funnel would increase bureaucracy, delay research submissions when often the timescale was very tight, and punish the innocent just because of the actions of one individual. The miscreant made things worse by claiming that his perceived sins were 'nothing to do with him' (the head of department), that he had 'done nothing wrong' and that 'this department has done nothing for me', when a good many of his colleagues felt equally strongly that the department had done far too much for him at the expense of others. The RAEs have made it unlikely such 'individualism' will go unchecked in future.

The impact of research on teaching

It always used to be assumed, or even asserted, that quality research informed quality teaching. Research results were fed into lectures, tutorials and seminars. Without sound, or better still, outstanding research, teaching would be poor and students would have a raw deal. To us, the most worrying aspect of the RAE is its apparent negative effect on and downgrading of teaching. McNay reminds us that

Research has a prestige premium over teaching for both individuals and institutions: a legacy of the concept of a university
developed over the past 50 years in the UK. The kudos attached
to research grades becomes part of individual identity more
so than high ratings for teaching. . . . The financial rewards to
institutions for quality teaching are non-existent in England
so there is a disparity of recognition in resource terms. Inevitably, that is reflected in internal reward systems despite efforts
in some institutions to adopt measures to counter it. Staff work
within the system.

(McNay 1997: 21–2)

He continues:

With the growth in student numbers but constrained resource,
teaching is becoming casualised or proletarianised. The new
elite, therefore, have structural enclaves with their research
students and assistants as acolytes. A separate career structure
for researchers is also emerging with agreement between the
Committee of Vice Chancellors and Principals (CVCP) and
research councils on terms and conditions of employment for
younger researchers and progression to readerships and heads
of research units now more built in to career planning.

(McNay 1997: 10–11)

So has the RAE made it even more difficult for high quality teachers,
administrators and 'good old workhorses' (who may well have taken
a great deal of weight off the star researchers) even less chance of
promotion post-RAE? It would seem likely. Has it really had such a
significant downgrading of the highly skilled and very demanding
job of teaching?

The proletarianization of teaching?

During the course of our research, we spoke to many academics,
particularly scientists and technologists, who categorically denied
that teaching had been downgraded. They claimed that they invariably drew on their own and other published research in order to
illustrate and illuminate theory. We have no cause to doubt their
word, but there is growing evidence of increasing numbers of retired
academics being re-employed in order to undertake large amounts
of teaching and other duties, to free the active researchers from such

time-consuming tasks. Moreover, numbers of postgraduate students are now being allocated lecturing, tutorial and examination marking duties. This may, or may not, indicate a downgrading of teaching. The practice of using large numbers of postgraduate teaching assistants is common in North America. If they are thrown in at the deep end, without support and without supervision, it would certainly be a worrying development, but if the preparation, briefing, training, support and supervision are sound, as has been found on occasions during the course of quality assessment visits (reported later in this chapter), the participation of postgraduate students might well be helpful to them in career terms, and at worst should be doing little harm to their students. However, too many teaching assistants and too few professors in the classroom are beginning to result in vociferously expressed student anger in certain prestigious American universities; this student disquiet should serve as a lesson of what can go wrong if teaching really is 'casualized or proletarianized', and if senior staff reduce or even opt out of teaching commitments.

Academic staff responses to the RAE

So what about the individuals who have participated? McNay's interviewees outlined three distinct responses by academic staff:

- *the positive*, who welcomed it as a recognition of their role and efforts, particularly where participation was for the first time and researchers could 'come out of the closet'. Such people would be competitive, proactive and would start to sell themselves and increase productivity;
- *the calculative*, who would 'play the game' and use their RAE status as a negotiating base, giving priority to research over teaching because of the rewards: 'I do what I need to get by in teaching' said one academic. In some cases tactics could involve choice of the unit of assessment (i.e. the department) with which to align;
- *the negative*, who would feel threatened and go into denial.

(McNay 1997: 16)

Whatever the response, and whether staff came into the positive, the calculative or the negative category, all agreed that a massive amount of work was required in assembling all the evidence, and that an effective approach to consolidating research effort was needed, not only to be ready for the likely next RAE, but also in order to ensure that their departmental research records were in better shape.

So was it all worth the effort?

Well, the winners in the RAE competition emerged triumphant and with enhanced status, but at a financial and personal cost. There is little doubt that it was stressful for everyone involved – those striving to maintain or improve their position, and particularly so for those institutions which started with a low grade, and considered it was desperately important to improve their rating in the next round. It undoubtedly resulted in more efficient management of research and went a long way to eliminate the near anarchic state of affairs which formerly prevailed in a few departments.

Research achievements have been brought into public view and the antics of the few individuals who felt they had no loyalty to anyone but themselves have been constrained, though the really cunning who are determined to buck the system will generally find ways of doing so. It brought increased research funding to universities and, with luck, to departments and that was a strong incentive for departments to pull out all the stops in order to achieve the best possible grade.

When it was all over, most of those involved would no doubt have taken a deep breath, sorted all the paper, restored order to their offices and hoped to be able to get on with routine work. But there was to be no guarantee of four years of calm reflection before the next RAE. Staff of subject-specified departments also had to face the reality of the quality assessment exercises, which carried no direct financial reward.

Teaching quality assessment

One of the criticisms of the quality audit is that it deals with procedures but its teams do not venture into the lecture or seminar rooms. The assessment teams make judgements about the quality of the student learning experience, which involves direct observation of teaching, (HEFCE 1997: 6). There have been some changes in procedures over the years, but the main elements have remained largely the same throughout.

The drawing of the quality assessment short straw

When the first assessments took place, selected departments which had only just completed the 1992 RAE submission may well have felt they had drawn the short straw. Professor Predmore, a senior professor of wide experience, and the head of one of the early departments to be assessed, recalled his weariness at having to go through the whole process of assembling documentation all over again. The prospect of having lectures, seminars and even tutorials observed was similarly unwelcome. His department had achieved the top grade in the RAE, and had always claimed, justifiably, to be a research focused department in a research focused university. 'Then,' he said, 'we had to prove we were good at everything else. That was not only much harder, but it required us to write down what we did and how we did it. That seemed to us to be a waste of valuable time.'

To make matters worse, the day notification was received that his department was to be assessed, he received a letter from the vice-chancellor which said, 'Get yourself off to be trained to be an assessor. We'd better get to know what this is all about.' Speaking much later to a group of academics who were themselves preparing for assessment, he said, 'My VC at that time was not a man to whom you could say "I am most honoured, sir, that you have selected me to put forward my name for training as an assessor, but I am rather busy just now and so, with great regret, I have to decline your kind invitation". You touch your forelock and you say, "Of course. I shall apply for consideration today". And I did.'

The first departmental meeting

As soon as the criteria for assessment were received, a full staff meeting was called in order to discuss what had to be done. In what had become the customary start to meetings, the first hour was spent on complaints on the lines of 'After all we had to do for the research assessment . . . As if we've nothing better to do than this . . . Who are these assessors anyway? What do they know about it all? Frankly, I believe we should just decline to participate' and 'I can't do anything about it. My priorities are to get on with my research'.

Professor Predmore said later that it was this last contribution which made him seriously angry. He knew the complaints script very well. He had heard it many times before, and from the same people, but on this occasion, the quality assessment was a departmental priority, not an individual research priority. He decided at that point that he was going to *make* everybody show some loyalty to the department for once, even if it resulted in full scale revolution.

Gathering the evidence for the RAE had been a nightmare. At first, he had assumed there would be a general willingness to demonstrate to the world that they were superb researchers, but the colleague who was given the task of coordinating returns was faced with every conceivable reason why some individuals could not possibly deliver the requested information on time, accurately referenced and in the required format. In the end, he had had to come to the aid of the despairing coordinator, to threaten and become seriously disagreeable. Even then there were defaulters.

He had learnt his lesson from the RAE experiences and was not about to allow a similar state of affairs to take hold.

> I decided I should have to take charge of the preparation myself and that I might as well start by being seriously disagreeable rather than waiting until we were in a mess. No democracy. No opting out. We had a job to do in a short space of time and we all had to take our fair share of the work. I was prepared to coordinate, to lead the campaign, to deal with delayers and excusers, but everybody had to be involved. I had no intention of doing all the work myself.

He decided it would be sensible to work through some of the items listed in the guidelines. He elected to start with the area he knew they were good at. They prided themselves on the way they looked after, encouraged and supported their students. He said, 'Right. Now then, what about student support? What precisely do we do to support our students?' An uncomfortable silence followed, until one senior lecturer said 'Well, they all know where I am. If they want anything, they can always come and find me'. It was at that moment that it became apparent that rather more work was required than had at first been anticipated. Things became even more worrying when they moved to curriculum organization, design and delivery. It seemed that no one was entirely clear what that meant.

Throughout Professor Predmore's years as a don in one of the UK's most prestigious universities, the term 'curriculum' was never mentioned. Teaching was allocated by means of courteous chats on the lines of, 'Oh, by the way, are you OK for third year mechanics?' Invariably, the response would be 'Yes. Of course.' Then part of the way through the academic year, someone would say 'Oh, will you let me have four questions for the third year mechanics exam by Thursday?' to which, as always, the response would be, 'Yes. Of course'. Not quite curriculum organization, design and delivery but as far as the smooth running of the department was concerned, it seemed to work all right. Unsuccessful attempts to disentangle what 'curriculum organization, design and delivery' meant in the context of their departmental provision set off the grumbles once more. The general feeling was that 'We do a good job, student evaluations are invariably positive, external examiner reports are always complimentary and students achieve good degrees, so what is the point of all this unnecessary paper work? We are doers in our own specialist fields, not educational theorists who just theorize'.

The problem facing Professor Predmore at this stage was that he agreed with them. The greater problem was that he knew they had no choice but to go along with the assessment and to do well, not least because if they did badly he would have to account for himself with the vice-chancellor. He had not enjoyed cordial relations with him in the past and had no wish to cross swords again. There was nothing for it. Battle stations had to be established.

The declaration of war

Staff claimed that he set about preparing for the assessment as if he were planning the equivalent of a more efficient version of the Battle of Waterloo. A full day away from the university was devoted to identifying areas which required clarification, analysis – and work. A gap analysis was carried out. Once gaps had been identified, groups of three were given specific tasks which had to be completed in a short space of time. No one was exempt. Tasks, names and report dates were listed on flip charts. Working on the assumption that more would need to be done after the first report back, time was allocated for possible slippage, but there had to be good reason for slippage. The law was laid down in a way that brooked no opposition.

The final date for reporting back was fixed; no one was left in any doubt that their tasks had to be completed and vetted by that date. Professor Predmore had changed character overnight. Gone was the pleasant 'I believe professionals should be allowed to get on with their job without interference' head of department. It was a case of 'You'll do this' and 'You'll do that'. It was as if he was nursing old angers and was oblivious to anyone's objections.

The war room

One of the remarkable aspects of the campaign was that after the original staff meeting and the planning day, there were no more meetings until the final reporting session. The task force trios were required to post their findings on charts fixed to the walls of a requisitioned tutorial room, which was open at all times for staff and for students. Some members of staff had at first opposed the access to students regime, fearing the addition of ribald comments (or worse), but that never happened. What did happen was that on a few occasions students added comments such as 'That is not true. That may be what you think happens, but it doesn't', followed by perfectly reasonable suggestions as to how things might be set right.

That was a surprise to everyone because there existed what staff had considered to be a cordial staff–student forum at which griev-ances could be aired. On no occasion had any student raised any of the issues which now appeared on the charts, but comments on the charts were anonymous, and anonymous comments are very different from public pronouncements in staff–student gatherings.

Another outcome of the open visiting to what came to be known as the war room was that some of the quiet workers came into their own. On numerous occasions when a gap in services or pro-vision had been noted on the chart, a note was added to the effect that X or Y had always dealt with that, and had records to demon-strate the what, the why and the when. Coffee conversations were on the line of

'Well, we can't claim we do anything about that, so we'll have
   to list it as one of those gaps we can't fill just now.'
'Yes, we can.'
'Can we? Well, who deals with it?'
'Ian. He always has done.'
'Really? Well, I never knew that. Why didn't he tell anybody?'

The war room charts had never been intended to be used as witch hunts. However, students had no inhibitions about naming mem-bers of staff who were always willing to listen, and to help in sort-ing out problems – and those who were not. They informed the task force trios which members of the department helped students who were struggling with their work, and those who pacified landlords who were threatening to evict them. What caused the greatest turmoil was that some postgraduate students signed their names to a statement indicating which individuals regularly assisted students whose theses were supervised by others who had a somewhat casual view of the role of doctoral supervisor. The students saw their opportunity to make their voices heard. They listed many strengths, but the war room charts also revealed weaknesses which set Professor Predmore on the warpath again. As one member of staff later said

> That war room was an eye-opener. Those charts really did rattle our cage. We might have been a bit arrogant, but the kind of things that emerged were pretty humbling. We'd never regarded Mark Predmore as a tyrant before, but he demonstrated increasingly formidable tyrant tendencies during the assessment preparation. We were all 'required' to spend at least five minutes each day reading, correcting and adding comments to the charts, and we began to feel he had probably installed secret cameras to check we did. In fact, the charts proved to be invaluable. We all learnt a lot.

The outcomes of the exercise

The department was given a top grade for teaching, to add to the top grade for research, which pleased everyone. The preparation for the assessment visit had revealed that in fact, a great deal of good work was being done, but there was very little coordination and so not everyone knew what was happening. Long held assumptions had been challenged and it had become apparent where individual loyalties lay. It certainly cleared the air and resulted in a fairer allocation of what one irate individual referred to as 'tiresome duties which will merely get in the way of my research'.

The assessors had observed teaching and that was a first-time experience for almost all academic staff. They had not enjoyed it, but in retrospect, most felt the experience of discussing their approach with an assessor was helpful. Thereafter, peer observation of teaching became part of the annual performance review. Professor Predmore's subsequent experience as a member of an assessment team convinced him of the value of observing the way other departments managed their affairs. From his early position of irritation and an attitude of 'Let's just get this thing out of the way and then we can get back to work', he became an enthusiast.

After all the charts had been removed and the war room returned to normal duties, he was asked whether he knew his staff had called him a tyrant, and that they looked forward to the return of their old style *laissez-faire* leader who let everybody do as they liked. He replied:

> They called me worse than that, but my approach was quite deliberate. Times have changed and I think I must have been living in the past. Over the years, I had become used to the minority of objectors, the time-wasters, the 'I'm too busy to do that-ers'. I think I just used to turn off and wait until they'd finished. I'm ashamed to say that too often I gave jobs to a few people because I knew they would do them well and too often allowed those who I knew would do jobs badly to get away with it. That won't happen again. The 'fair shares for all' routine of this assessment preparation worked well, even though some of them never stopped moaning.

Asked whether the new structures and procedures would now be forgotten, he said,

> No. They won't. This exercise made us identify what we did well, but it brought to light serious gaps in our practice. It drew attention to all sorts of things that we assumed we did – or at least, we assumed someone was doing. We'd never have carried out that really fundamental and time-consuming enquiry without the threat of the assessment. There would always have been what we considered to be more important things to do. We now have better structures in all areas of our work and that should make life easier for us to keep up to date. We mustn't let them slip. In future, we should be able to cope with anything that hits us. I'm a researcher by inclination, but this experience made me think about what my job of head of department is.

He finished by saying,

> I think we were fortunate with our assessment team. We could talk to them as equals. I showed them the charts and I wouldn't have done that with people I didn't trust. It did us no harm to talk about our deficiencies. It might have been different with another team. As it was, it did us a lot of good. Not everybody

agrees with me though. Quite a few of them still think it's all been a complete waste of time.

He was asked what he, personally, had learnt from the experience. He found that difficult but, honest to the end, he said:

I found the experience quite shaming, to the extent that I discovered I really did not know enough about what was going on in my own department. I knew what research people did, and I assumed that the teaching was done at the times it should be done, but this exercise brought into the open just how much responsibility some people carried in ensuring that our students were well looked after. They tended to be the ones who were sometimes doing a very large amount of teaching and tutorial work, but not always a great deal of research. They had been overlooked in the glory stakes, and that was my fault.

The impact of the quality assessment exercise

The *Report on Quality Assessment 1995–1996* (HEFCE 1997) stated:

the overall picture that emerges from the assessments is highly positive, but there is also clear evidence of where and how improvement may be needed. The great majority of students are receiving a high quality education. In nearly all assessments, subject providers demonstrate high achievement in meeting the aims and objectives that they set for the education of their students.

(HEFCE 1997: 6)

In general, our informants agree with this judgement, though unfortunately we have not been able to obtain responses from departments which were rated at a lower level than they had hoped. They might well have had less positive views.

However, examples of the impact of the assessment exercises are beginning to emerge on a variety of fronts.

The willingness of journals and newspapers to pass on the bad news of any 'unsatisfactory' judgements has done much to concentrate the mind of some vice-chancellors who, in general, do not like their institutions to be seen as anything other than first class. Reports are now available on the Internet and comments have been received from several thousand students on the lines of 'The team got it right. Those changes are needed'. The HEFCE now has to decide how to respond to them, if at all.

One university department of English (one of the few rated 'unsatisfactory') had the dubious pleasure of having its many deficiencies listed on the front page of *The Times Higher Education Supplement* of 29 September 1995. As a result, two masters courses were immediately closed. In our view, that one case should be justification enough for the continuation of the quality assessment exercise and it is to be hoped that the swift action has served as an example to any other sinners.

There are dangers though. It now appears that 'satisfactory' ratings are not enough for some vice-chancellors, who regard anything less than 'excellent' as the equivalent of abject failure. We have heard of threats of budget cuts and demands for major structural and staffing changes, including downgrading, compulsory early retirements, long term sick leave and course closures. Whatever next? Are these reported cases coincidental? Or were they the direct result of quality assessment visits? No one is willing, or able to say categorically that they were, or were not, though staff of the departments concerned have no doubt what triggered such hard-hitting actions.

One interesting side-effect of the quality assessment initiative has been its value to the assessors themselves, well over 80 per cent of whom are staff of universities or colleges of higher education, the remainder being drawn from industry, commerce, the professions and private practice (HEFCE 1997: 36, para. 131). Quality assessment is a peer review system and training for assessors is very thorough. This in itself must be valuable in-service training. However, the main value to the individuals concerned and to their departments lies in the experience gained by being full members of assessment teams. There is now a growing body of evidence to indicate that assessors are able to take back to their own institutions examples of alternative, and often better ways of planning and delivering curricula. Around 1500 academics have now been through different types of assessment training, and feedback from them leaves little doubt as to its value.

A waste of everyone's time or real value for money?

These three exercises have had a major influence on working practices in higher education, though in very different ways. In the prestige pecking order, research heads the list, and there are no signs that this position will change – at least, not in the foreseeable future. Quality research brings in significantly more funding than quality teaching and it puts individuals in line for promotion when so far, few institutions have rewarded star teachers. The RAE has resulted in a number of changes in the management of research at departmental level and it appears to have produced a degree of order, planning and establishment of priorities. It has certainly increased the amount of research being done in universities, and it may have improved the quality (though opinions are divided on that score). Certainly grades have improved overall.

The downside of the RAE is, or certainly appears to be, the downgrading of teaching, but the introduction of the quality assessment exercises has to some extent taken steps to balance departmental priorities. We have less evidence of the effectiveness of the audits, though the presence of an experienced team and their guidance about ways in which practice might be improved must often have served as a valuable, and relatively inexpensive consultancy exercise.

Whatever their influence, the assessments and the audits will continue until the year 2001, when the newly established Quality Assurance Agency (QAA) will assume overall responsibility for the monitoring of all quality assurance in institutions of higher education, though exactly how has yet to be decided. In the meantime, it is business as usual, or at least, almost as usual until 2001.

The changes anticipated in the new QAA regime have made two universities question the point of continuing with the audits, at least until news is received about the form the model will take. In 1997, twenty-seven universities were invited to take part in an audit update. Two of those invited, Cambridge and Birmingham, declined to participate. In a letter to the HEQC, a spokesman for Birmingham University was reported as saying that

> it would be a great pity if you went ahead now, only to find that the format of the continuing audit was significantly altered in the light of the requirements of a new single quality assurance organisation. It would be even more of a pity if it were decided that a separate audit process was unnecessary.
>
> (*The Times Higher Education Supplement* 27 July 1997)

The HEQC was particularly concerned that Cambridge had declined to participate as the last report on the university, published in July 1992 'revealed some significant weaknesses'. We have no way of knowing whether those 'weaknesses' were ever addressed, but if the audits continue to be on an invitation basis, rather than a requirement, with penalties for defaulters, we can only presume that the two decliners have a perfect right to opt out. It is perhaps surprising that more have not followed suit, and as audit and assessment fatigue increases, there just could be more resistance to the workload involved.

These three initiatives have certainly provided a general shake-up, but have they really been worth the very considerable cost to the Exchequer, and the even greater cost in terms of the stress and fatigue experienced by individuals involved in one, two or even in all three of these exercises? The two departmentally based initiatives – the quality assessment and the RAE – necessarily involved almost every member of the departments concerned. In the most effective examples, this participation resulted in team building activities and the development of a culture of departmental loyalty. Unfortunately, not all departments can claim so much.

Some of those involved still complain that they know full well what their strengths and weaknesses are; that they would have tightened up procedures, monitored the quality of teaching, increased and improved research, without any external intervention. Perhaps they would. However, in very many institutions, we suspect there would have been little incentive for hard pressed departments to face up to known (or even unknown) inadequacies had there not been external monitoring of performance and the publication of 'no punches pulled' reports. Departments are genuinely very busy and tasks relegated to the 'when we have time' or 'too hard' tray would inevitably have been delayed for another day, week, year – or for ever. It would seem we all need some form of compulsion, threat or reward before we can ever find the time to do what would be desirable, but not exactly essential – at least, not just now.

It will never be possible to equate improvement in students' learning experience with financial outlay. Much has to be taken on trust, and the value, or otherwise, of these exercises may well take several years to become apparent. However, during the course of our interviews, it has seemed to us that a great deal has been achieved which would have had little chance of receiving any priority without a strong push from funding or other bodies. Individuals, institutions and departments have been forced to become aware of the implications of poor practice. Serious sinners have been punished in various ways, deficiencies have been made known to the world and, in some cases, swift action demanded to eliminate them. Some of the quiet workers have been brought in from the cold, and the nature of their contributions to students and to their departments recognized.

Institutional and departmental leaders and managers have had their skills tested to the full, and not all have been equal to the challenge. However, valuable lessons have been learnt, and unless the ever-increasing demands on time and patience push these lessons into the ' perhaps when I have time' file, they should serve as a reminder that it is generally as well to try to learn from experience.

Postscript

One of the senior professors who read the draft of this chapter gently rebuked us for implying that curriculum planning in universities was, at best, haphazard. He wrote: 'My own experience is rather different. It may be because I work in a strongly multidisciplinary department but courses and programmes are reviewed very regularly. I suspect this partly results from pressure from individuals to make sure their particular subject gets a full slice of curriculum time, but nevertheless the days of "Oh, are you all right for third-year mechanics" are long gone – at least in our case.'

He also queried our view of the employment of early retirees being employed to relieve the research active from 'such time consuming tasks' as teaching. He pointed out that 'increased student numbers, wider ranges of courses, accredited programmes having requirements for a range of professional inputs mean that extra staff are required. Funding for full time appointments is not available. Moreover, in my experience, these people are usually very good teachers and their students benefit from their having more time for preparation'.

The second professor/reader provided the following comments on what he saw as the different approaches to the management of the teaching quality assessment and the research assessment exercises:

Overall, I believe that the TQA process can be managed by heads of department more easily than the research assessment because it is, or should be, a straightforward organizational matter – as long as student support, teaching, and everything else are in good shape. The RAE and the enhancement of departmental research is not a straightforward matter of management.

Because research is a creative activity, it needs enthusiasm and commitment from those doing it.

I believe the RAE requirements generally help vice chancellors and heads of department who need to bring everyone on board in a research-active sense. The assessment procedures mean that those who put up a research smokescreen but actually produce nothing now have nowhere to hide.

Finally, there is the question of the impact of research on teaching. My own experience is that the good researchers are generally good teachers and that their teaching is enhanced by their research.

Clearly experience varies, but in our view, there is little doubt that where research and teaching really are complementary and mutually reinforcing, students are likely to be the winners.

9

TOWARDS A NEW

PROFESSIONALISM:

EXPLOITING A RESOURCE?

OR SERVING PEOPLE'S REAL

NEEDS?

This chapter considers how the quest for continuous improvements of staff can, yet need not, involve continuous exploitation of staff. It draws on a major study of secondary school leaders' experience of professional development. All principals and their staff must now work in more open conditions, where the 'secret garden' of professional privilege is being replaced by a more open, professional identity. Educational leaders know that they need to be highly skilled in self-aware leadership for staff and students, and in their relations with all interlinking school–community groups, including parents, employers, support agencies, tertiary institutions and others.

Self-aware leadership links with the ideal of lifelong learning for all. A crucial component of principals' expertise will be their ability to generate similar high levels of leadership among all their staff, who will all become members of learning teams. Professional development for school leaders will involve effective provision for themselves, for all staff, and for all students, to become career-long continuous learners. Through this, a concern for the personal well-being of individuals and teams in the school becomes inseparable from a concern for continuous school improvement.

In pursuing their quest for success, schools and college leaders who recognize the importance of continuous learning and development for their staff, know too that they must share in this process and become not only 'leaders of learning', but also 'leaders in learning' (Munro 1997: 2). Long gone, we trust, are the days when principals might have compared themselves to circus ring masters, who train the circus troupe to perform in the ring according to instructions. The learning quest is, like the quest for success itself, now a shared quest.

That, at least, is the vision; yet, when times are bad, the vision may well seem as elusive as ever. The spirit of the Investors in People initiative (discussed in Chapter 6) was to regenerate a trust that people can improve their organizations by taking opportunities to improve themselves. This spirit has been international and inter-organizational, and has grown steadily in scope. The personal well-being of people, in addition to their professional effectiveness, is now seen to be crucial to the organization's own well-being. Writing on 'Warming the cold heart of business', for example, Dutton (1997: 18) identifies the growing importance of loyalty to employees, as well as to customers, to ensure the survival and prosperity of business. Following an era of downsizing, cost cutting, merges and consolidation, 'companies are searching for the heart of their businesses and finding it in their employees'. They are developing programmes that aim to 'take some of the pressure off workers' personal lives and with policies that allow greater employee autonomy. The pay off comes through increased worker loyalty, enhanced productivity and, sometimes, reduced sick leave and health care costs'. In short, good managers recognize that good ethical practice is good business: 'loyalty of a company to its employees, of employees to a company, builds trust, and trust goes hand in hand with profitability' (Dutton 1997: 20).

Through their classroom and staffroom experience, any good teacher knows that as long as there is a firm commitment to the task, the climate of encouragement and goodwill will greatly enhance successful learning and action. Similarly, school leaders can inspire the whole climate of a school if they can share their own positive approach to their work.

But who helps the principal to get it right?

In an Australian context, three school leader professional associations (primary principals, secondary principals, secondary deputy principals) formed a cooperative research partnership with a university, in order to identify current critical issues in the professional development of school leaders. While Australia has witnessed a number of innovative links between universities and schools for teacher professional development (see Currie 1996), this partnership represented a new way of bringing together these major stakeholders in school leaders' professional development. The initiative worked to remove that sense of isolation in which individual bodies traditionally acted, with all the dangers of poor communication, misunderstanding and even hostility which accompany isolation. As is shown in Hill *et al.* (1997), collaboration characterized all stages of the research, from the design of research instruments, through to analysis and presentation of findings.

Exploratory interviews with senior representatives of the school leader associations produced rich insights into the ways that these 'leaders of leaders' operated within their own schools. As might be expected, these select principals had an especially high charge of energy. Valerie, for example, claimed: 'I love my school; I love the energy and I love the drive of the teachers and the students'. Using a familiar Australian analogy, this principal compared her role to that of a team coach, then as a team supporter:

> I am more or less a coach, or a person who is quite available.
> . . . I talk to my staff, and try to share with each of them. So I
> guess that sort of fostering, the open approach, is what I try to
> do – establish that rapport with people so that they can say
> whatever is on their mind and be up front about it. I see
> myself as a person to support the resource needs of teachers,
> so that they can do their job. I also see myself as a barracker of
> the teachers and of the school – a supporter.

The attitude expressed by Valerie about her staff is one of wholehearted immersion in their work, and absorption in their progress. This exemplifies a view of leadership that is, in Duignan's (1997: 7) terms, 'anchored firmly in the here-and-now – in the hearts, minds, and souls of her staff'. Duignan continues, 'these leaders are more sensitive and caring in their attitudes and relationships and more adaptable and flexible in their practice. They release the potential, and tap the diversity of talents of those who work with them'. A key feature of authentic leaders is that they are also good learners, and educative leadership 'promotes a culture of sharing in which authentic relationships are valued' (p. 9). Developing his theme of 'a thirst for learning, a holy curiosity, a commitment to the dance of learning', Duignan examines group dynamics in terms of the poet Coleridge's observation of a flock of starlings, which moved with 'harmony and synchronization, but they were unpredictable in terms of constancy of direction and shape of the flock. They performed the dance, however, acting as a social relational whole' (p. 15). In drawing an analogy with people movements, Duignan suggests that it is advisable to observe but not to interfere in such complex behaviour:

> Change is too often approached through restructuring or fiddling with external indicators. During restructuring or downsizing the shape of the flock is often mandated from above but the individual members are not consulted and/or do not understand (or perhaps agree with) the new rules for flocking. No real attempts are made to understand what is making individual members fly . . . individuals are seldom asked about their views on the meaning of flocking and on how the creative spirit and the individual can be protected, even encouraged, while still preserving the positive aspects of flocking. The result is, of course, that the whole flock may perish through misadventure or, more likely, individual members ignore the new rules, no real learning takes place and nothing actually changes at all.
>
> (Duignan 1997: 16–17)

This powerful metaphor of movements among a flock of starlings, to convey the 'dance of relationships' in team work, reveals the importance of integrating clarity of purpose with harmony of interaction among a whole team. Too often, let us admit, reality falls far short of the ideal here, in the daily lives of organizations, since it is notoriously true that a team can only be as strong as its weakest link. Yet weak links can be strengthened, and leaders have a human, as well as an organizational obligation, to do all they can to support strengthening, before reverting to the much less pleasant (though sometimes necessary) option of discarding a link. Michael, an experienced and successful secondary principal, reflects on an important point in his own career, when he had to confront dysfunction in his school team:

The only negative spots occur when the relationships among staff are negative and difficult, and you have few allies to be able to push forward. . . . Unless you have the support of people around you, you cannot really grow, nor can you do much. I did have a very difficult situation in one school where there was a very negative group, but I was young and confident, stepping into it there, and I was able to manage that and effect some changes myself. Perhaps naivety is a strength in some ways; you have this idealism and zeal, and you go through with it. You burst through it. It did not stop me.

Michael acknowledged, though, that the blind confidence of naivety must be short lived. When he was reminded that he had gained a considerable reputation (which went far beyond his own school) for successful leadership through good relationships and team work, he commented:

Well, I do enjoy, genuinely enjoy seeing other people get satisfaction. I get an enormous amount of fulfilment out of seeing other people have satisfaction, and that to me is important. I'm interested in others, I listen to others, I'm interested in their growth points and I encourage growth points. I'm not a power player and I'm not ambitious, nor do I want to get only personal kudos. You know, I like acknowledgement, but I don't want to have it at the expense of others. I would rather achieve kudos through other people. I have an enthusiasm for things and for others and this is appreciated, and therefore they get caught up in it. You know, they enjoy being in an exciting situation. I think that is a factor.

This enlightened view, of what it takes to become an effective professional leader, shows how individuals are, themselves, part of a historic process, through both their own personal and professional maturation, and also through the larger evolutions of organizations and whole societies. During the decades in which Michael has served as a principal, these larger movements have led to changing notions of what it is to be a professional educator. Reflecting on this, Michael disclosed that he could never, in his own view, have been a 'charismatic' leader. He had, he thought, 'been very lucky in that there's been the change in the style of leadership from the authoritarian to the leader who more suits my personality. I was born at the right time. I came just at the right time'. He had been able to build 'very strong professional relationships' with people who shared his deep interest in education. He was 'quite amazed that my friends are people who tend to be those who are innovative and interested in education', and who took major leadership roles within the secondary school service. In short, Michael interpreted his degree of influence in terms of things achieved, not of personal reputation. Although Michael was not acquainted with the 'starling flock' analogy for team leadership, he understood its import at once. It encapsulated, he thought,

> our rationale in terms of multiple leaders and multiple learners. Everybody is a leader and we operate within systems works units, or teams of people who interact with one another and are accountable to one another. There is not the line management dependency – really, I feel line management just blocks so much advancement opportunities; as long as we know what the general principles are for the school's operation and we are helping students, we are moving more towards them in learning philosophy . . . we have had very few backlashes in terms of decisions made here, because there is adequate consultation, there is opportunity to be involved. If you don't want to be involved, you delegate to other people and then it is always in a formative or developmental stage. You're not saying finally, 'right, this is it'. We will always be alert to changes and make modifications. So, yes, every exercise is a learning exercise. I'm very keen not to create 'them and us' situations. I want everybody to be in the process, the learning process, moving and advancing in the general direction we want to pursue, based on good information. It is good information that we want to work on, so I work on a principle of data based decision making or information based decision making, and the information comes from a wide variety of sources.

The decisions made by the teacher teams, which developed in Michael's school, match the decisions of the starling flock, in that both are based on best information that can be communicated by any individual member of the team or flock. That continuous responsiveness to information, or research evidence, ensured maximum sensitivity and flexibility in making essential adjustments of direction in policy and practice. However, Michael's commitment within his own school to research information was not always shared by educational leaders and administrators outside the school. To his dismay, he found an 'anti-research' climate among some senior colleagues ('you know we don't want research'), which left him 'really just flabbergasted'. Even though these senior people knew there was major change ahead, there was not just resistance, but downright hostility to research questions even being raised (for example, on issues of school discipline). Yet, despite any individual's or group's or organization's resistance to information and research evidence, the environment around them will continue to change. How, then, can educational leaders prepare themselves for present and future conditions?

Towards a new professionalism

As has been seen, Michael's version of principalship operates within a new framework of accountability and consultation throughout the school. Having realized that his professional authority can no longer rely on being unconditionally 'authorized' by traditional bureaucracies or religions or other fixities, he decided to rethink what it means to be a professional educator. In doing so, he was able to show how school educators may best develop new capabilities that will enable them to fulfil their important mission in schools. An important shift of focus involves the word 'professional' itself – a term which has long been problematic.

As with other long lived notions, 'professionalism' has gathered a cluster of associations, which may often be contradictory, from various past traditions. Professionalism can imply, for example, exclusive possession of expert knowledge, for example in law, medicine or other fields. It might involve an agreed code of ethics and behaviour in dealing with professional clients. It can still be used to distinguish between 'amateur' (unpaid) and 'professional' (paid) activities in work or sport. The call to behave 'professionally' is sometimes invoked as a means of exploiting already overworked groups – such as teachers (Blackmore *et al.* 1996: 202; Hargreaves 1997). Or it may, for some, imply little more than a comfortable lifestyle that includes protected employment and salaries, power dressing and power language, and privileged access to goods and services.

Seeking to clarify issues here, Hargreaves (1997) proposed that educators should, by now, have moved beyond the notion of 'professional'. He traces developments from professional to collegial, through to post-collegial, in order to examine changing relations between educators and the communities that they serve. Others, such as Nixon *et al.* (1997), have sought to redefine 'professional' in a postmodern world. In a study which traces the shifting notions of professionalism over more than a century, the Nixon team argue for a 'new professionalism', which will transcend traditional notions of professionals as acknowledged civic leaders whose authority was not to be disputed. Their proposal for a new version of teacher professionality is based on 'the enabling of learning, the accommodation of difference, and the practice of agreement' (Nixon *et al.* 1997: 5). 'Difference' may be social, cultural or philosophical; 'agreement' has to be worked for, and must 'extend to parents and students' (p. 25). There is every reason, arguably, for the 'agreement' to be extended to all education stakeholders in the community. Guided by an ethics of integrative action, the new professionalism will be performed by 'dissolving the traditional distinction between professional and non-professional' (p. 25). This need not mean, however, that professions will lose their distinctive identity, nor their freedom to make choices. As Broadbent *et al.* (1997: 10) point out, the new professional 'cannot be simply told what to do, whom to identify with, and how to change', since organizations will be seen increasingly, in terms of multiple identities and interests.

We acknowledge the useful ground work in redefining 'professional' in this and other work by Nixon *et al.* (1996; 1997). What, then, might the reconstructed term mean for practising school leaders? In the Australian context, at least, it informs them that decision making in education cannot remain exclusively in the domain of a state or national education authority. Pressures have grown steadily during the 1990s to weaken the traditional powers of education authorities (as happened in the UK and elsewhere). At the same time, school leaders have also had to accept that their own traditional, largely unquestioned authority has also come into question. Increasingly, they must see themselves in a negotiating role with their education authorities, with government and community bodies and attitudes, with parents, and (perhaps least familiarly of all), with the experiences and views of their own students. In short, this is already, in both senses, a post-authoritarian era; it is not a comfortable time for many principals, who understand, more sharply than their observers and critics may manage to do, that their task is to resolve competing and often contradictory interests among those who would seek to influence them.

Covey (1990) suggested that the reasons why people do not change, even when they realize that change is right, are that (a) they are not hurting enough, and (b) they don't want to change their lifestyle. Can we, though, look to a controlled evolution, without the disruption that massive change can produce (such as, for example, through the sudden dismantling of bureaucracies), to achieve the new professionalism and, with it, a continuous improvement in schools?

The danger of wholesale disruption does not only arise in countries which are experiencing unprecedented rates of change, such as South Africa or India. In the comparatively settled context of the UK, for example, even enthusiastic advocates for market reforms in education such as Jones (1996: 134) have admitted that the swift introduction of market mechanisms to drive change has produced costs of 'uncertainty, disruption and transition throughout the education sector'. Similar warnings emerged in Canada (Fullan 1993; 1995), Australia and elsewhere (Gronn 1996; Townsend 1996). Since school leaders are, above all, concerned with the present and future well-being of people, they need favourable conditions, as well as special expertise, to ensure that their professional management of people is sensitive to all the conditions of those with whom they deal.

New capabilities for school leaders

Commenting on the excessive zeal to impose change, that some educational policy makers showed in the 1980s, Fullan (1991: 7) warned about serious limitations in the concept of the principal as 'lead implementor of official policies and programmes', and that educational research was, itself, in danger of 'unintentionally reinforcing dependency'. Government and community expect principals to lead change that will bring about visible and lasting improvement in schools. Yet government and community have also asserted a right to intervene on educational processes, to ensure that principals toe the line of central policies.

Principals, suggested Fullan (1991: 38), need sometimes to resist, as well as accommodate such pressures: 'the focused, interactive, interdependent principal is a socially responsible being, working avidly on the improvement of the school'. This emphasis on interaction was developed by Fullan and Hargreaves (1991: 106); they emphasized that 'interactive professionalism must be laced with cross-school and extra-district contact'. During the 1990s there has been a drive, among professional and academic educators, to redefine roles for school leaders and their senior management teams.

This drive had a particular aim to achieve continuous school improvement (see e.g. Bell and Harrison 1995; Fullan 1995). With varying degrees of emphasis, these reinforce the argument of Nixon's team, that the means of achieving goals are no less crucial than the ends themselves. A vital aim in improving schools is, after all, to improve the quality of human life – in the present, as well as in the future.

What means, in particular, do these educators identify? Throughout this book, we have argued that the post-authoritarian professional needs, above all, to have 'people qualities' – to have high levels of interpersonal skills, and to lead by example. School leaders should be well informed as should all professional groups; a great deal will depend on their ability to make informed, critical judgements. Yet they should also be alert to the dangers of judgement being lost under too much unsifted information.

New professional educators work in a 'high involvement framework', where teachers may feel, in the words of a primary school teacher, that 'we've really been developed. We highly regard professional developments . . . I've never stopped learning since I've been here' (quoted in Odden and Odden 1996: 166). Thus the vision of a continuous learning organization is already becoming realized through the work of such teachers, and there is no lack of useful advice on practical implementation. It is on the innovative efforts of such practitioners that the vision must depend, for enactment. As Bennis (1996: 157) has suggested, successful innovators in any sphere are 'pragmatic dreamers – men and women whose ability to get things done is often grounded in a vision that includes altruism'.

As a practising secondary school principal in Western Australia, Robin Clarke worked with his staff to devise, for whole school use, a statement on whole school development which incorporates principles for the continuously learning organization. The statement (Belmont Senior High School 1996/7) incorporates the school's purpose to develop the whole person both as a 'happy self-reliant individual and as an effective and responsible member of society'. The dual purpose – to link personal well-being with the quest to develop effective citizens – is incorporated in a vision which celebrates cooperation: see Figure 9.1.

This vision is student centred rather than directed towards actual staff development as such. Yet the import for significant professional development of teachers is clear, if the staff are to achieve all the learning outcomes that this school seeks for its students. Fourteen learning outcomes were identified, which aim to ensure that all students can

- communicate effectively in English
- handle mathematical concepts and processes
- find and use information
- utilize technology effectively

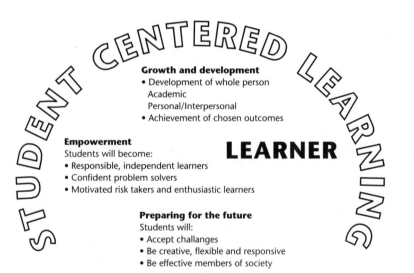

Working in teams
Will:
- Provide sense of 'belonging'
- Promote sharing and joint decision making
- Enhance continuity of learning
- Enhance positive relationships

Participative decision making
Will provide opportunities for:
- Involvement of all key interest groups
- Listening to one another
- Getting things done together

Growth and development
- Development of whole person
  Academic
  Personal/Interpersonal
- Achievement of chosen outcomes

Empowerment
Students will become:
- Responsible, independent learners
- Confident problem solvers
- Motivated risk takers and enthusiastic learners

LEARNER

Preparing for the future
Students will:
- Accept challanges
- Be creative, flexible and responsive
- Be effective members of society

Curriculum
Will be:
- Relevant, meaningful and negotiated
- Provide access and opportunity for all
- Provide developmental approach which is outcomes based

Learning environment
Will feature:
- Caring, sensitivity and responsiveness
- Development of self worth and equal opportunity for all
- Energy, enthusiasm and commitment
- Professional practice
- Innovation

Figure 9.1 Our vision

- work both independently and cooperatively
- have an approach to learning which is critical, reflective and responsive
- have the creative, logical and enterprising skills necessary to solve problems
- understand their society and environment and have skills necessary to be informed, responsible citizens
- understand the natural world and are able to apply scientific concepts and processes
- have the capacity to appreciate the arts and to express their creativity
- have the understandings and skills necessary to achieve health and well-being
- communicate in a language other than English
- have respect for the rights of others
- value themselves as learners.

The whole school development plan, by which the school will enact the vision and aims for learning outcomes, reveals the importance of both inter-school and intra-school cooperation: see Figure 9.2.

The practical steps in this school plan reflect sound principles in both school leadership and in cognition processes of learning. Mason (1996), for example, has demonstrated the importance of 'collaborative reasoning', in fostering conceptual growth in understanding phenomena. Halpern (1997), too, has argued that teaching must incorporate 'an understanding of the way in which learners represent knowledge internally, and the way in which these representations resist change when learners encounter new information'. What is true of school students is true of all groups, including the staff and parents of any school. They need to have appropriate conditions in which they can help each other to become changed through learning, and in which they may also 'remain flexible enough to recognize new paradigms' (Halpern 1997; see also Nichols 1996).

It is through collaborative interaction that visions and values are actualized. This provides an essential means through which potentially conflicting values (among teachers themselves, as well as among parents and students) may be understood, then resolved. People are disposed to infer their own meanings from experience, then to impose those meanings on the world (Ormrod 1995: 307). In the face of this, school leaders should review whether they are communicating well enough with the various groups whom they

School operations
- Occupational health and safety
- Managing student behaviour review
- Attendance review
- Executive

Staff support
- Staff assembly
- Professional development
- Induction
- Performance management
- Executive
- Senior staff council

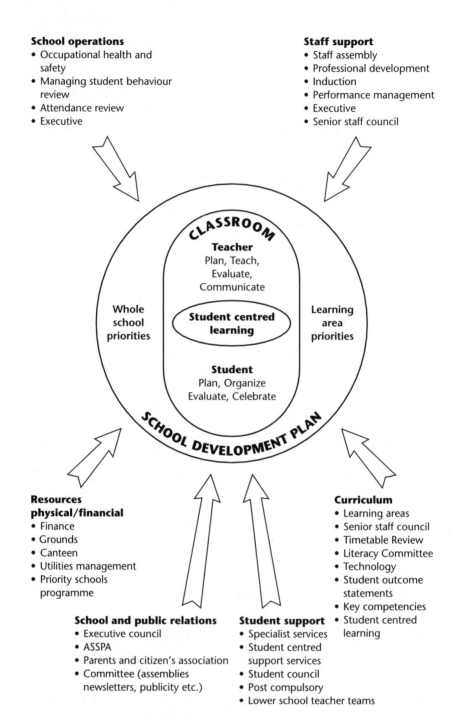

CLASSROOM

Teacher
Plan, Teach, Evaluate, Communicate

Whole school priorities

Student centred learning

Learning area priorities

Student
Plan, Organize Evaluate, Celebrate

SCHOOL DEVELOPMENT PLAN

Resources physical/financial
- Finance
- Grounds
- Canteen
- Utilities management
- Priority schools programme

Curriculum
- Learning areas
- Senior staff council
- Timetable Review
- Literacy Committee
- Technology
- Student outcome statements
- Key competencies
- Student centred learning

School and public relations
- Executive council
- ASSPA
- Parents and citizen's association
- Committee (assemblies newsletters, publicity etc.)

Student support
- Specialist services
- Student centred support services
- Student council
- Post compulsory
- Lower school teacher teams

Figure 9.2 Decision making groups

serve. Principals, suggests Hince (1997: 38), need to move beyond 'telling', to taking responsibility for the 'creation of meaning', on behalf of those who would listen. This involves considering the experiences of others, capitalizing on these by presenting ideas in terms of their listeners' experiences, and compensating for any gaps of understanding that may exist (Hince 1997: 40). This is true of all, not just educational relations. Reflecting on commercial organizations, Kets de Vries declared: 'the derailment of a chief executive officer is seldom caused by a lack of information about the latest techniques – rather, it comes about because of a lack of interpersonal skills – a failure to get the best out of people who possess necessary information' (quoted in Levinson 1996: 158).

Even so, school stakeholders look to school leaders to provide their distinctive expertise, as do all professional clients. Increasingly, for example, schools need to develop their own access to research and evaluation findings which have a direct impact on their own school. This will enable them to resist the crude impact of, for example, national school league tables that rely on raw external examination results, or other generalized data. In order to manage school improvement through problem solving, they need to be able to receive information from large scale research/evaluation findings, that is appropriate to their own actual needs, or the particular needs of parents and others involved in a particular school (Nahra 1997: vii). Furthermore, they need to develop their own research and evaluation instruments within the school; this process will, itself, involve significant professional development and cooperation with other agencies, such as university education faculties and state departments of education (Fitzgibbon 1996; Harrison 1996).

Identifying needs for the new professionalism

The Belmont Vision and Plans for decision-making teams (Figures 9.1 and 9.2) reflect the principal's mission to share common purposes in working with staff and students. As the Japanese industrialist Morita (1987: 12) pointed out, it is important to 'make use of the motivations you share with people to accomplish something that will be to the advantage of both'. Morita's accompanying comment on being a boss also carries a message to policy makers, politicians and, indeed, school leaders and their staffs: 'don't think that because you are at the top you can boss others around'. The Belmont School Plan worked through a strong sense of common purpose, and was lodged in an essentially democratic framework which seeks 'power speak' (Brodeth 1997) for all.

The sense of common purpose in this school became, then, a vital part of its culture; and culture, as Pepper (1995: 31) has claimed, 'is pervasive. It is not simply a variable that affects the organization, it is indistinguishable from the organization'. For Pepper, a focus on culture is 'a focus on the routine, on the everyday sense-making that is the process of building a sense of shared reality'. Yet it includes, also, 'a focus on the official, or the everyday contrived attempts to build identity and manage relationships'. Cultural development, in short, might seem to be a natural evolution, but it depends on the determined efforts of those who lead. In Conrad's (1994: 27) view, once the right cultural climate is established, it can then be 'sustained by the communicative acts of all employees, not just the conscious persuasion strategies of upper management. Cultures do not exist separately from people communicating with each other'. Commenting on this process at Belmont, the principal described how individual teams are 'self-initiating, self-organizing, self-managing and self-evaluating – and this occurs at lots of different levels'. For example, the whole area of teaching in the school is a critical field for professional leadership growth. In this area,

> most of the team leaders, interestingly, have not been in promotional positions. They have been mainly young people who were doing such a terrific job that they had virtually grasped the agenda, they have taken this over from their heads of department, not deferring to them; here is a leadership growth opportunity just for the asking. If they nominate, they generally get the job; it is a very demanding job because they have got to manage teachers, students, parents and curriculum for 50 or 60 students over two years.

It is not surprising that a principal should look to younger staff, to lead those new teams, where flexibility is of the essence. Having acknowledged that, though, the real art in setting up these teams might lie not only in recruiting the young, but also keeping them young, and ensuring regular rejuvenation throughout a teaching career.

In this chapter we have drawn on accounts by practising principals, who are succeeding in their exacting task of motivating people to improve schools through improving their own performance. These principals share a fresh view of educational professionalism, which engages them in continuous networking, consultation and collaboration with their staff and all those involved with the school. They also share in common a disposition to be firm about tasks that need to be done, yet they offer goodwill and fairness in their daily dealings with colleagues. They believe that their colleagues have the potential to be at least as good as themselves. They also accept that they have an important role in ensuring that staff have fair opportunities to develop their potential. Above all, they lead by example, in developing a new course of educational professionalism among their staff. This includes, we were glad to note, a sense of delight and celebration in their own professional lives, and in the achievement of their staff and all members of the school community.

POSTSCRIPT

The cases described and discussed in the nine chapters of this book illustrate the range of issues facing education professionals, and the way some of the people involved responded to demands for change. There are few educational institutions anywhere in the world which have not now been required to be more accountable, more efficient and to do more for less money – and most chapters illustrate the way people in their various ways interacted, coped (or in a few cases failed to cope) and learnt from their experience of adjusting to change.

As Harvey-Jones (1988: 1) reminded us in Chapter 1, there are no quick-fix solutions; no 'instant prescription, which if followed will solve every ill from bankruptcy to athlete's foot', because we are dealing with people, who are likely to react in different ways to different situations. Even so, all our anonymous contributors strongly believe that reflecting on their experience taught them valuable lessons about themselves, their own actions and the actions of others in times of crisis – and as a result, as one of them said, 'should enable me to learn from the past in order to be able to operate more effectively, and more sensitively, in the future. The job has to be done, the economies have to be achieved, but I hope I shall never forget that people matter. I think for a short time, I was under such pressure that I almost forgot that.'

REFERENCES

Adams, K. (1996) Making capital out of Investors in People. *IRS Employment Review: Employee Development Bulletin* 84, 622 (December): 11–16.

Anderson, E. (1995) The idea of education and the culture wars, Melbourne Winter Conversazione for 1995. Melbourne: Boston, Melbourne, Oxford Conversazione on Culture and Society.

Arcaro, J.S. (1995) *Teams in Education: Creating an Integrated Approach.* London: Kogan Page.

Association of European Universities (1997) *Restructuring the University: Report on Universities and the Challenges of New Technologies.* Limerick: University of Limerick.

Auld, R. (1976) *William Tyndale Junior and Infants Schools Public Enquiry.* London: Inner London Education Authority.

Ball, S.J. (1987) *The Micro-Politics of the School: Towards a Theory of School Organization.* London: Methuen.

Ball, S.J. (1994) *Education Reform: A Critical and Post-Structural Approach.* Buckingham: Open University Press.

Barratt-Pugh, C., Breen, M.P., Kinder, J.J., Rohl, M. and House, H. (1996) *Learning in Two Languages.* Belconnen: Language Australia.

Bell, D. (1997) An evaluation of the effectiveness of the gap model as a framework for assessing the quality of higher education. *Journal of Institutional Research in Australia* 6, 2: 35–46.

Bell, J. (1996) An investigation into barriers to completion of postgraduate research degree students in three universities. Unpublished report funded through the Leverhulme Emeritus research fund.

Bell, J. and Harrison, B.T. (eds) (1995) *Vision and Values in Managing Education: Successful Leadership Principles and Practice.* London: David Fulton.

Belmont Senior High School (1996/7) *Belmont Senior High School Development Plan.* Belmont, Perth: Belmont Senior High School.

Bennis, W. (1996) 'The leader as storyteller' (review of H. Gardner and E. Laskin, *Leading Minds: An Anatomy of Leadership*). *Harvard Business Review* Jan–Feb: 154–60.

Blackmore, J., Bigum, C., Hodgens, J. and Laskey, L. (1996) Managed change and self-management in schools of the future. *Leading and Managing* 2/3: 195–220.

Bottery, M. (1995) Education and quality: is a 'business perspective' enough?, in J. Bell and B.T. Harrison (eds) *Vision and Values in Managing Education.* London: David Fulton.

Broadbent, J., Dietrich, M. and Roberts, J. (eds) (1997) *The End of the Professions? The Restructuring of Professional Work.* London: Routledge.

Brodeth, E. (1997) Women in leadership. Public lecture. Perth: Edith Cowan University (October).

Caldwell, B. (1997) Thinking in time: a Gestalt for schools in the new millennium, in B. Davies and L. Ellison (eds) *School Leadership for the 21st Century: A Competency and Knowledge Approach.* London: Routledge.

Chan Kim, W. and Mauborgne, R. (1997) Fair process: managing in the knowledge economy. *Harvard Business Review* July–Aug: 65–75.

Charlton, R. and Dewdney, M. (1995) *The Mediator's Handbook. Skills and Strategies for Practitioners.* Sydney: Law Book Company.

Coleman, L. (1997) Businessmen, pollies relinquish duty of care. *The Australian* 23 April.

Conrad, C. (1994) *Strategic Organizational Communication: Towards the Twenty-First Century*, 3rd edn. Fort Worth, TX: Harcourt Brace.

Coulson-Thomas, C. (1997) *The Future of the Organisation: Achieving Excellence through Business Transformation.* London: Kogan Page.

Covey, S.R. (1990) *The 7 Habits of Highly Effective People: Restoring the Character Ethic.* Melbourne: Business Library.

Currie, J. (1996) *Reflection in Action: School Reform and Professional Learning through Collaboration Inquiry. A Portrayal Evaluation of the Innovative Links Project for Teacher Professional Development, ACIIC Roundtable, University of Sydney.* Murdoch, WA: Innovative Links Project.

Day, A. (1992) Aboriginal students succeeding in the senior high school years: a strengthening and changing Aboriginality challenges the negative stereotype. *Australasian Journal of Gifted Education* 40/1: 14–26.

Dearing, R. (1993) *The National Curriculum and its Assessment (The Dearing Report).* London: School Curriculum and Assessment Authority.

Dent, J.D. and Hatton, E. (1996) Education and poverty: an Australian primary school case study. *Australian Journal of Education* 40/1: 46–64.

DfEE (Department for Education and Employment) (1997) *Investors in People and School Self-Improvement*. London: DfEE.

Dolence, M.G. and Norris, D.M. (1995) *Transforming Higher Education*. Ann Arbor, MI: Society for College and University Planning.

Drucker, P.F. (1977) *Management*. New York: Harper's College Press.

Duignan, P. (1997) *The Dance of Leadership: At the Still Point of the Turning World*. ACEA Monograph Series 21. Victoria: ACEA (Australian Council for Educational Administration).

Dutton, G. (1997) Warming the cold heart of business. *Management Review: American Management Association* June: 17–20.

Eastcott, L.R. (1996) 'Possibilities and constraints: lessons from the past and the present for change into the 21st century.' Unpublished paper presented at the AAIR (Australian Association for Institutional Research) International Conference, Brisbane.

Eisenhardt, K.M., Kahwajy, J.L. and Bourgeois III, L.J. (1997) How management teams can have a good fight. *Harvard Business Review* July–Aug: 77–85.

Employee Development Bulletin (1992) Investors in People. *Industrial Relations Review and Report* 520 (September).

Engeström, G. (1994) Teachers as collaborative thinkers: activity-theoretical study of an innovative teacher team, in I. Carlgren, G. Handal and S. Vaage (eds) *Teachers' Minds and Actions: Research on Teachers' Thinking and Practice*. London: Falmer.

Evans, D. and Panacek-Howell, L. (1995) Restructuring education: national reform in regular education, in J. Paul, H. Rosselli and D. Evans (eds) *Integrating School Restructuring and Special Education Reform*. Fort Worth, TX: Harcourt Brace.

Finn, E. (1994) Investors in People: counting the dividends. *Personnel Management* 26, 5: 30–3.

Fitzgibbon, C.T. (1996) *Monitoring Education*. London: Cassell.

Fullan, M. (1991) *What's Worth Fighting for in the Principalship? Strategies for Taking Charge in the School Principalship*. Victoria: Australian Council for Education Administration.

Fullan, M. (1993) *Change Forces: Probing the Depths of Educational Reform*. London: Falmer.

Fullan, M. (1995) *Reshaping the Teaching Profession*. Melbourne: Incorporated Association of Registered Teachers in Victoria.

Fullan, M. and Hargreaves, A. (1991) *Working Together for your School: Strategies for Developing Interactive Professionalism in your School*. Victoria: Australian Council for Educational Administration.

Gray, Lynton (1984) Managing resources in schools and colleges', in S. Goulding, J. Bell, T. Bush, with A. Fox and J. Goodey (eds) *Case Studies in Educational Management*. London: Harper & Row, in association with the Open University.

Grogan, M. (1997) Why educational leaders should develop relationships based on care, Charlottesville Conference on Values and Leadership, Charlottesville, Virginia (October).

Gronn, P. (1996) Time to take stock? *Leading and Managing* 2/3: ii–iii.

Halpern, D. (1997) The ways of the worlds: when students' conceptual understanding clashes with their professors. *Chronicle of Higher Education* XLIII, 27: B5.

Halsey, A.H. (1992) *The Decline of Donnish Dominion.* Oxford: Oxford University Press.

Handy, C. (1993) *Understanding Organisations,* 4th edn. Harmondsworth: Penguin.

Handy, C. (1994) *The Empty Raincoat: Making Sense of the Future.* London: Hutchinson.

Handy, C. (1995) *Beyond Certainty: The Changing Worlds of Organizations.* London: Hutchinson.

Hargreaves, A. (1997) The four ages of professionalism. Conference on the Status of Teaching. Melbourne: Australian College of Education (May).

Hargreaves, A. and Goodson, I.F. (1995) Teachers' professional lives: aspirations and actualities, in I.F. Goodson and A. Hargreaves (eds) *Teachers' Professional Lives.* London: Falmer.

Harrison, B.T. (1995) Revaluing leadership and service in educational management, in J. Bell and B.T. Harrison (eds) *Vision and Values in Managing Education: Successful Leadership Principles and Practice.* London: David Fulton.

Harrison, B.T. (1996) *Researching Education: Making Meanings to Make Better Schools.* Perth: Edith Cowan University.

Harrison, B.T. (1998) Managing pastoral care in schools: taking responsibility for people, in M. Calvert and J. Henderson (eds) *Managing Pastoral Care: Policy and Practice.* London: Cassell.

Harrison, B.T., Dobell, A. and Higgins, C. (1995) *Self-Determining Managers: Evidence from Senior Managers in Educational and Other Organizations.* University of Sheffield: Teacher Development Research Centre.

Harrison, B.T., Wyatt, K. and Partington, G. (1997) *School Retention, Motivation and Achievement amongst Adolescent Aboriginal Students: an Enquiry into Successful Practice.* Collaborative Research Study, Edith Cowan University/Education Department of Western Australia (EDWA), funded by Australian Research Council/EDWA.

Harvey-Jones, J. (1988) *Making it Happen: Reflections on Leadership.* London: Collins.

HEFCE (Higher Education Funding Council for England) (1997) *Report on Quality Assessment 1995–1996.* Bristol: HEFCE.

Heifetz, R.A. and Laurie, D.L. (1997) The work of leadership. *Harvard Business Review* Jan–Feb: 124–34.

HEQC (Higher Education Quality Council) (1994) *Guidelines on Quality Assurance.* London: HEQC.

Herriot, P. (1992) *The Career Management Challenge: Balancing Individual and Organizational Needs.* London: Sage.

Hill, S., Clarke, R., Harrison, B.T. and Harvey, M. (1997) *School Leaders Professional Development Survey. Stage 1: Survey Report.* Perth: Faculty of Education, Edith Cowan University/Western Australian Primary and Secondary Principals' Associations (WAPPA/WASPA).

Hince, R. (1997) 'I told them – but they didn't understand'. The importance of oral communication. *Practising Administrator* 19, 1: 38–40.

Hopson, B. and Scally, M. (1981) *Lifeskills Teaching.* London: McGraw-Hill.

Hough, M. and Paine, J. with Austin, L. (1997) *Creating Quality Learning Communities.* Melbourne: Macmillan.

Hoyle, E. (1982) The micropolitics of educational organizations. *Educational Management and Administration* 10, 2: 87–98.

Hoyle, E. (1986) *The Politics of the School.* London: Hodder and Stoughton.

IIP (Investors in People) (1995) *Investors in People: The Case Studies.* London: IIP.

IIP (1996) *Revised Indicators: Advice and Guidance for Employers.* London: IIP.

Irwin, B. (1996) *Leaders in Australia: The Australian Cultural Imprint for Leadership.* Warrandy Ee, Victoria: Cultural Imprint.

Johnson, G. (1992) Managing strategic change – strategy, culture and action. *Long Range Planning* 25, 1: 28–36.

Jones, G. (1996) The British experience of reform in education. *Journal of Higher Education Policy and Management* 18, 2: 125–37.

Kaku, R. (1997) The path of Kyosei. *Harvard Business Review* July–Aug: 55–60.

Kalliopuska, M. (1990) Self-esteem and empathy as related to participation in the arts or sports activities, in L. Oppenheimer (ed.) *The Self Concept: European Perspectives on its Development, Aspects and Applications.* Berlin: Springer-Verlag.

Kanter, R.M. (1983) *The Change Masters: Corporate Entrepreneurs at Work.* London: Unwin Hyman.

Kanter, R.M. (1989) *When Giants Learn to Dance: Mastering the Challenges of Strategy, Management and Careers in the 1990s.* London: Simon and Schuster.

Kenfield, J. (1997) A transforming experience. *Inter-Act: IINCM Newsletter* 2, 1: 2.

Krell, T.C. and Spich, R.S. (1996) A model of lame duck situations in changing organizations. *Journal of Organizational Change Management* 9, 4: 56–68.

Kuhn, T.S. (1970) *The Structure of Scientific Revolutions,* 2nd edn. Chicago: University of Chicago Press.

Lawrence, B. and Hayden, C. (1997) Primary school exclusions. *Educational Research and Evaluation* 3, 1: 54–78.

Leonard, D. and Straus, S. (1997) Putting your company's whole brain to work. *Harvard Business Review* July–Aug: 111–21.

Levine, A. (1997) Higher education's new status as a mature industry. *Chronicle of Higher Education* 43, 21: A48.

Levinson, H. (1996) The leader as analyst (review of M.F.R. Kets de Vries, *Life and Death in the Executive Fast Lane*). *Harvard Business Review* Jan–Feb: 158.

Lingard, B. (1996) Educational policy making in a post modern state: on Stephen J. Ball's *Educational Reform: A Critical and Post-Structural Approach*. *Australian Educational Researcher* 23, 1: 65–91.

McNay, I. (1997) *The Impact of the 1992 Research Assessment Exercise on Individual and Institutional Behaviour in English Higher Education: Summary Report and Commentary*. Anglic Polytechnic University: Centre for Higher Education Management.

Maeroff, G.I. (1993) *Team Building for School Change: Equipping Teachers for New Roles*. New York: Teachers College Press.

Maloney, J. (1996) Improving your expression of anger. *Human Development* 17, 4: 26–9.

Marginson, S. (1996) University organization in an age of perpetual motion. *Journal of Higher Education Policy and Management* 18, 2: 117–23.

Mason, D.A. and Burns, R.B. (1997) Reassessing the effects of combination classes. *Educational Research and Evaluation* 3, 1: 1–53.

Mason, L. (1996) Collaborative reasoning on self-generated analogies: conceptual growth in understanding scientific phenomena. *Educational Research and Evaluation* 2, 4: 309–50.

Mellaville, A.I. and Blank, M.J. (1991) *What It Takes: Structuring Interagency Partnerships to Connect Children and Families with Comprehensive Services*. Washington, DC: Education and Human Resources Consortium.

Møller, J. (1996) Reframing educational leadership in the perspective of dilemmas, reproduced, with permission, in L. Kydd, M. Crawford and C. Riches (1997) *Professional Development for Educational Management*. Buckingham: Open University Press.

Moodie, G. (1997) Working 9 to 5 – we wish. *The Australian* 29 October: 42.

Morgan, G. (1988) *Riding the Waves of Change: Developing Managerial Competences for a Turbulent World*. San Francisco, CA: Jossey-Bass.

Morita, A. (1987) *Made in Japan*. London: Collins.

Munro, J. (1997) *'Leaders of Learning as Leaders in Learning': Hot Topics, no. 2*. Victoria: Australian Council for Education Administration.

Murgatroyd, S. and Morgan, C. (1992) *Total Quality Management and the School*. Buckingham: Open University Press.

Nahra, C. (1997) Farewell to the rule of thumb. Multimedia section, *The Times Higher Education Supplement* 14 March.

Nichols, J.D. (1996) Co-operative learning: a motivational tool to enhance student persistence, self-regulation, and efforts to please teachers and parents. *Education Research and Evaluation* 2, 3: 246–60.

Nicholson, R. (1997) *Chancellor's installation address*. Perth: Edith Cowan University (February).

Nixon, J.B.T. (1997) Regenerating professionalism within the academic workplace, in J. Broadbent, M. Dietrich and J. Roberts (eds) *The End of the Professions? The Restructuring of Professional Work*. London: Routledge.

Nixon, J., Martin, J., McKeown, P. and Ranson, S. (1996) *Encouraging Learning: Towards a Theory of the Learning School*. Buckingham: Open University Press.

Nixon, J., Martin, J., McKeown, P. and Ranson, S. (1997) Towards a new professionalism: changing codes of occupational practice within the new management of education. *Journal of Sociology of Education* 18, 1: 5–28.

Noddings, N. (1995) Teaching themes of care. *Phi Delta Kappa* 76, 7: 675–9.

Odden, A. and Odden, E. (1996) Applying the high involvement framework to local management of schools in Victoria, Australia. *Educational Research and Evaluation* 2, 2: 150–84.

Ormrod, J.E. (1995) *Educational Psychology: Principles and Applications*. Columbus, Ohio: Merrill.

Ow Yong Kean Guan (1995) Formation years in Japan's school system: towards the foundation of nation-building. *Jurnal Pengurusan Pendidikan* 5, 1: 48–54.

Parasuraman, A., Zeithaml, V.A. and Berry, L.L. (1990) *Delivering Quality Service: Balancing Consumer Perceptions and Expectations*. New York: Free Press.

Partington, G., Harrison, B.T., Godfrey, J. and Wyatt, K. (1997) Why is it important for Aboriginal students to stay on at school and succeed? Factors in the process of dropping out and pushing out of Aboriginal secondary students. Australian Teacher Education Association National Conference, Yeppoon, Queensland (July).

Pepper, G.L. (1995) *Communicating in Organizations: A Culture Approach*. New York: McGraw-Hill.

Peters, T.J. and Waterman, R.H. (1982) *In Search of Excellence*. New York: Harper and Row.

Petterle, J. (1993) *Schools Flunk – Kids Don't*. Glendale, CA: Griffin.

Pilger, J. (1989) *A Secret Country*. London: Jonathan Cape.

Pollard, A. and Tann, S. (eds) (1993) *Reflective Teaching in the Primary School*, 2nd edn. London: Cassell.

Pring, R. (1997) *Closing the Gap: Liberal Education and Vocational Preparation*. London: Hodder and Stoughton.

Ranson, S. and Stewart, S. (1994) *Towards a Theory of Public Management: Management for the Public Domain – Enabling the Learning Society*. London: Macmillan.

Senge, P.M. (1994) *The Fifth Discipline: The Art and Practice of the Learning Organization*. New York: Currency Doubleday.

Souter, K.D. and Stearman, K. (1988) *Aboriginal Australian*. London: Minority Rights Group, Report no. 35.

Spilsbury, M. and Stone, S. (1995) Attitudes to Investors in People: 1994 employer survey. *Labour Market Trends* November.

Spilsbury, M., Atkinson, J., Hillage, J. and Meager, N. (1994) *Evaluation of Investors in People in England and Wales*, Report no. 263. Brighton: Institute of Manpower Studies.
Stokes, K. (1997) Enterprise in Australia: the risks and rewards, the 1997 Herbert Cole Coombes Lecture. Perth: Edith Cowan University.
Teacher Training Agency (TTA) (1997) *National Professional Qualification for Headship: High Quality Training for Tomorrow's School Leaders*. London: TTA.
Telford, H. (1995) Collaborative leadership in inner city Schools in Melbourne, in R. Cotter and J.E. Marshall (eds) *Research and Practice in Educational Administration*. Victoria: Australian Council for Educational Administration.
Tinkler, D., Lepani, B. and Mitchell, J. (1996) *Education and Technology Convergence*. National Bureau for Education, Employment and Training (NBEET) Commissioned Report no. 43. Canberra: Australian Government Publishing Service.
Tjosvold, D. and Tjosvold, M.M. (1991) *Leading the Team Organization: How to Create a Competitive Advantage*. New York: Macmillan.
Tomlinson, H. (ed.) (1992) *Performance-Related Pay in Education*. London: Routledge.
Townsend, A. (1996) The self-managing school. *Leading and Managing* 2, 3: 171–94.
Venables, J. (1997) Burn out warning at rebirth of the cool. Multimedia section, *The Times Higher Education Supplement* 14 March.
Wallace, M. and Hall, V. (1994) *Inside the SMT: Teamwork in Secondary School Management*. London: Paul Chapman.
Wasley, P. (1994) *Stirring the Chalkdust: Tales of Teachers Changing Classroom Practice*. New York: Teachers College Press.
West-Burnham, J. (1992) *Managing Quality in Schools*. Harlow: Longman.
Whitaker, P. (1997) The personal dimension, in *Managing Change in Schools*. Harlow: Longman.
Wood, G. (1993) *Schools that Work: America's Most Innovative Public Education Programs*. New York: Penguin.
Yetton, P. and associates (1997) *Managing the Introduction of Technology in the Delivery and Administration of Higher Education*. Canberra: Department of Education, Employment, Training and Youth Affairs (DEETYA).
Yoshida, R. (1994) Beyond the alternative of 'compulsion' or 'freedom': reflections on the Buber–Rogers dialogue, in D.M. Bethel (ed.) *Compulsory Schooling and Human Learning: The Moral Failure of Public Education in America and Japan*. San Francisco: Caddo Gap.

INDEX

LEADING PRIMARY SCHOOLS
THE PLEASURE, PAIN AND PRINCIPLES OF BEING A PRIMARY
HEADTEACHER

David Clegg and Shirley Billington

- How can headteachers retain a set of principles and values in the face of a myriad of external demands and expectations?
- What is the nature of leadership in the primary school?

This book is intended for headteachers or those who aspire to headship in primary schools. Through a reappraisal of the nature of headship, the book explores the complex nature of the job, and in particular the many paradoxes which confront primary headteachers on a day-to-day basis. The authors place the job of headship firmly in the context of attitudes and values and argue that many of the management orthodoxies which have permeated education are unhelpful or inappropriate in primary schools. The book examines the various dimensions of headship and focuses particularly on the nature of educational leadership and the importance of developing successful working relationships.

Contents
Introduction – The paradox of headship – The myth of the manager – What does it mean to be a headteacher? – The rhetoric of school development planning – Defining the purpose – Working with staff – Working with parents and the community – Summary – Bibliography.

128pp   0 335 19644 6 (Paperback)   0 335 19645 4 (Hardback)

WHAT'S WORTH FIGHTING FOR IN YOUR SCHOOL?
WORKING TOGETHER FOR IMPROVEMENT

Michael Fullan and Andy Hargreaves

This is about how to make schools more interesting and fulfilling places to be. It tackles how to bring about marked improvements in the daily lives and experiences of teachers, heads and pupils. The premise is that teachers and heads themselves should ultimately *make* this happen.

Almost everywhere, teachers and heads are overloaded and undervalued. Teachers and heads will need to take more of the initiative themselves, not just in holding off unreasonable demands, not just in bargaining for better conditions but also in making constructive improvements of their own, as a professional community. Examples of such constructive practice already exist but they need to be broadened, strengthened and developed. This book is meant to stimulate such improvements. It is a practical book and a provocative one; fully aware of the constraints and everyday problems facing teachers but clear in setting out what really is worth fighting for in schools.

No teacher or head will read this book without responding in the light of his or her personal experiences, beliefs and passion about teaching; and all will be challenged by this catalyst for action.

Contents
Preface to the British edition – Foreword – Acknowledgements – The authors – Introduction – The problem – Total teachers – Total schools – Guidelines for action – References.

160pp   0 335 15755 6 (Paperback)

LEADERSHIP AND TEAMS IN EDUCATIONAL MANAGEMENT
Megan Crawford, Lesley Kydd and Colin Riches (eds)

Effective leadership and team working makes a crucial difference to the management of schools and colleges. This book takes readers through the different dimensions of leadership, and its relationship to good team work. Personal and organizational skills are dealt with alongside the more theoretical aspects of the subject. Throughout, the editors stress that leadership and team working are the core activities in managing people.

This volume forms part of the *Leadership and Management in Education* series. This four book series provides a carefully chosen selection of high quality readings on key contemporary themes in educational management: professional development, reflection on practice, leadership, team working, effectiveness and improvement, quality, strategy and resources. The series will be an important resource for classroom teachers and lecturers as well as those holding designated management posts in schools and colleges and will provide a valuable basis for professional development programmes.

Contents
Introduction – Part 1: Leading and leadership – Leadership as an organizational quality – Dimensions of leadership – Primary headship and leadership – Critical leadership studies – Women in educational management – Motivation in education –Managing stress in educational organizations – Managing conflict in organizations – Part 2: Working in teams – Staff teams and their management – The dynamics of teams – Headship and effective teams in the primary school – Managers communicating – Communication in educational management – Effective teambuilding – Index.

208pp   0 335 19841 4 (Paperback)   0 335 19842 2 (Hardback)